IMPLANTED
UNIVERSES

KEYS TO THE KINGDOM SERIES
POCKET EDITION

THIS BOOK SHOULD NOT BE LEFT
ACCESSIBLE, IN CLEAR VIEW, OR
SHARED CASUALLY WITH OTHERS

Published from
Mardukite Borsippa HQ, San Luis Valley, Colorado
Mardukite Academy & Systemology Society
for spiritual or philosophical purposes only

IMPLANTED UNIVERSES

Systemology
Advanced Training Course
Manual #4

As presented by Joshua Free
to the Systemology Society

THE JOSHUA FREE IMPRINT
JFI PUBLICATIONS

This manual is restricted to students on
The Systemology Advanced Training Course
that have already completed the
"Pathway to Ascension" Professional Course

References to prerequisite material:
"The Secret of Universes" (AT #1)
"Games, Goals & Purposes" (AT #2)
"The Jewel of Knowledge" (AT #3)
"Eliminating Barriers" (PC-7)
"Conquest of Illusion" (PC-8)
"Spiritual Implants" (PC-11)
"Games & Universes" (PC-12)
"Spiritual Machinery" (PC-14)
"The Arcs of Infinity" (PC-15)

Full use of this manual may also require:
"Systemology Biofeedback" and
"Systemology Procedures"

<u>*Advanced Manuals should be studied in the*</u>
<u>*sequential order in which they are numbered.*</u>

First Edition Pocket Paperback — *March 2024*

mardukite.com

The Keys to the Kingdom are Yours for the Taking!

The official Mardukite Systemology "Advanced Training Course" is now available in print for the first time.

Those Seekers that have completed the "Pathway to Ascension" Systemology Professional Course can now access the upper-level teachings of our tradition.

This book is not for everyone...
This is the fourth manual for Level-7.

Never before has Joshua Free presented this material outside the confines of the Mardukite NexGen Systemology Society.

Learn how to expertly apply our spiritual technology toward reaching higher levels of Awareness and Beingness than ever before thought possible for humanity on planet Earth.

Each of the "Keys to the Kingdom" Advanced Training Course Manuals will further a Seekers reach on the Pathway leading out of this Universe.

The Pathway to Ascension
Professional Course Lesson Booklet Series

#1 – *Increasing Awareness (Level-0)*
#2 – *Thought & Emotion (Level-0)*
#3 – *Clear Communication (Level-0)*
#4 – *Handling Humanity (Level-1)*
#5 – *Free Your Spirit (Level-2)*
#6 – *Escaping Spirit-Traps (Level-2)*
#7 – *Eliminating Barriers (Level-3)*
#8 – *Conquest of Illusion (Level-3)*
#9 – *Confronting the Past (Level-4)*
#10 – *Lifting the Veils (Level-4)*
#11 – *Spiritual Implants (Level-5)*
#12 – *Games and Universes (Level-5)*
#13 – *Spiritual Energy (Level-6)*
#14 – *Spiritual Machinery (Level-6)*
#15 – *The Arcs of Infinity (Level-6)*
#16 – *Alpha Thought (Level-6)*

Keys to the Kingdom
Advanced Training Course Manuals

#1 – *The Secret of Universes (Level-7)*
#2 – *Games, Goals & Purposes (Level-7)*
#3 – *The Jewel of Knowledge (Level-7)*
#4 – *Implanted Universes (Level-7)*
#5 – *Entities & Fragments (Level-8)*

Advanced Training Supplemental Booklets

#1 – *Systemology Biofeedback*
#2 – *Systemology Procedures*
#3 – *Systemology Piloting*

TABLET OF CONTENTS

INTRODUCTION TO THE MANUAL

A.T. MANUAL #4:
IMPLANTED UNIVERSES

APPENDIX

"Many years ago, I realized that 'The Way Out' would systematically resemble the routes by which we originally descended."
—*Joshua Free*
Backtrack Lectures, 2023

INTRODUCTION TO
THE MANUAL

This manual is restricted to students on
The Systemology Advanced Training Course
that have already completed the
"Pathway to Ascension" Professional Course

References to prerequisite material:
"The Secret of Universes" (AT #1)
"Games, Goals & Purposes" (AT #2)
"The Jewel of Knowledge" (AT #3)
"Eliminating Barriers" (PC-7)
"Conquest of Illusion" (PC-8)
"Spiritual Implants" (PC-11)
"Games & Universes" (PC-12)
"Spiritual Machinery" (PC-14)
"The Arcs of Infinity" (PC-15)

Full use of this manual may also require:
"Systemology Biofeedback" and
"Systemology Procedures"

THE SYSTEMOLOGY ADVANCED TRAINING COURSE MANUAL SERIES

Mardukite Systemology is a new evolution in Human understanding about the "systems" governing *Life, Reality,* the *Universe* and all *Existences.* It is also a *Spiritual Path* used to transcend the Human experience and reach *"Ascension."*

This is an *Advanced Training* (*AT*) course manual detailing *upper-levels* of our spiritual philosophy. It is intended to assist *advancing* a *Seeker*'s personal progress toward the *upper-most levels* of the *Pathway.*

This manual follows after our *Professional Course* series of lessons—available as individual booklets, or collected in two volumes titled *"The Pathway to Ascension"* The *Professional Course* follows after material given in the *Basic Course* booklets, or *"Fundamentals of Systemology"* volume.

The systematic methodology that we use to assist an individual to increase their *"Actualized Awareness"* (and reach gradually higher toward their *"Spiritual Ascension"*) is referred to as *"The Pathway"* — and that individual is called a *"Seeker."*

To receive the greatest benefit from this manual: it is expected that a *Seeker* will already be familiar with the fundamental concepts and terminology (previously relayed in the *Basic Course* and *Professional Course* lessons) of our *applied philosophy.*

As a *Seeker* increases their *Awareness* in this lifetime, their spiritual *"Knowingness"* also increases—which is to say their *certainty* on *Life,* on this and other *Universes,* and on *realizing Self* as an unlimited "spiritual being" *having* an enforced restrictive "human experience." A *Seeker* also *knowingly* increases their command and control of the "human experience." And this is a part of what is meant by *"Actualized Awareness."*

CHARTING FLIGHTS ON THE PATHWAY

Although there is a systematic structure to *fragmentation,* the personal journey experienced along the *Pathway* will be different for each *Seeker.* For example, certain areas will seem more *"turbulent"* or difficult for one *Seeker* than another. We tend to say that these areas have more *"charge"* on them—or that they are more *"heavily charged."* It is best to handle such areas when you are already feeling "good" and not in a situation (or condition) where that specific area is consistently being *"triggered"* or *"restimulated."*

As an applied philosophy, *Systemology* "theory" can be easily utilized in the "laboratory" of the "world-at-large" in everyday life. This is implied within the basic instruction of each lesson. Unlike other "sciences" that conduct experiments by making a change to some "objective variable" *out there* and waiting to see an effect, our focus is the individual (or *Observer*) themselves, and how *they* affect the "*Reality*" perceived.

Our philosophy is applied by using specific exercises and systematic techniques. These "*processes*" provide the most stable personal gain (and *realizations*) for each area; but only when actually applied with a *Seeker's* full "*presence*" and *Awareness*. Hundreds of such *processes* may be found in the "*Pathway to Ascension*" (*Professional Course*) material.

Applying a technique is called "*running a process.*" *Processes* are designed with very simple instructions or "*command-lines.*" To *run* a *processing command-line*, a *Seeker* may be assisted by the communication of that *line* from a "*Co-Pilot*" (as in "*Traditional Piloting*"). But even then, a *Seeker* must still personally "input" the *command* as *Self*. For this reason—and quite thankfully—*Solo-Processing* is possible.

TAKING FLIGHT ON THE PATHWAY

Processing Techniques are intended to treat the *Spiritual Being* or *Alpha-Spirit*; the individual themselves. The *"command-lines"* are *directed to* the individual themselves—not some *mental machinery* of theirs, and not even a *Biofeedback* metering device.

Systematic Processing is applied by the *Alpha-Spirit*—who then *Self-directs* command of their "Mind-System" or "body" (*genetic-vehicle*), both of which are "constructs" that the *Alpha-Spirit* (*Self*, or the "I-AM" *Awareness unit*) operates, but neither of which is actually *Self*. *Fragmentation* causes *Humans* to falsely identify *Self as* the *"Mind"* or even a *"Body."*

Some *processes* can be treated quite lightly at first; others may require a bit of working at in order to get *"running"* well. It is important to set aside a period of time

when you can be dedicated to your stud-
ies and *processing*. This period of time is
referred to as a *"processing session."* When
a *process* does start *running* well, it is important to be able to complete it to a satis-
factory *"end-point."*

Processing allows us to be able to *actually*
"look" at *things* and even determine the
considerations we have made—or attitudes
we have decided—about *Reality* as a result of those experiences.

It doesn't do us much good to simply
"glance"—or to *restimulate* something uncomfortable and then quickly *withdraw*
from it once again, leaving more of our
attention yet again behind and held fixedly on it.

Generally speaking, a *Seeker* continues to
run a *process* so long as something is
"happening"—which is to say, the *process*
is still producing a change. Usually this is
evident by the type of "answers" that a

command-line prompts a *Seeker* to originate from the database of their own *Mind-System*.

Processing Command-Lines ("PCL") are not "magic words"; they do not "do" anything on their own. They systematically assist a *Seeker* to direct their own attention toward increasing *Awareness*.

A *Seeker* may also cease to generate new "data" from a *process* without reaching an *"ultimate" realization* as an *"end-point."* It is possible that additional "layers" (or even other "areas") require handling before anything "deeper" is accessible. If this is the case, end the *process*. But, if a *Seeker* is *withdrawing* from something uncomfortable that was incited or stirred up, then a *process* is *run* until they feel "good" about it.

One of the benefits to *Flying-Solo* on the *Pathway* is that the *processing* is entirely *Self-determined*. This naturally provides a certain built-in "safety" for a practitioner. Anything you *restimulate* by *Self-determinism* is *your thing*. It is not triggered or incited by some external *"other-determined"* influences (or other "source-points") that make you an *effect*. It can be more easily handled in *processing*—or you can simply let things "cool down" and come back to it again in another *session*.

While it may seem "mysterious" to beginners, a *Seeker* gets a sense for knowing how long to *run* a *process* only with practice. Once you have spent some time actually applying material from *"The Pathway to Ascension" Professional Course*, there are many aspects of it that become "second nature" because they are, in fact, a part of our true original native nature. All we have done in *Systemology* is *"reverse engineer"* the routes of *creation* and *consideration* that are already *our own*.

SYSTEMOLOGY LEVEL-7

We are publishing *"upper-level"* *Systemology* in 2024 for the very first time. Its application is dependent on a *Seeker* reaching a stable point of *"Beta-Defragmentation."* This requires proper use of materials for previous *processing-levels*—as given in the *"Pathway to Ascension" Professional Course*. Of course, we don't refer to such an individual as *"defragmented"*—which only further reinforces that *something* exists to *defragment*—but instead, as having reached a *Beta-state* of *Self-Honesty*. This "state" *must* be reached in order to go further.

Up to this point, a *Seeker* has become *"better-abled"* in the *game* of *"Being Human."* They have learned to play the *game* of *Beta-Existence* better—while still *on Earth*, and possibly still quite fixated on a

"Human Body." Yet, the completion of *Systemology Level-6* is still a stable point of accomplishment—and well above the level of *Awareness* maintained by the "standard-issue" *Human Condition.* The individual is less likely to fall into as many *traps* and is more able to "brush off" most additional *fragmentation* before it accumulates.

"Alpha-Defragmentation" is what the *"Keys to the Kingdom" Advanced Training Course* manuals pertain to. Our aim is still for *"metahuman destinations."* The goal of *Systemology Level-7* is to "safely" deliver (or *Pilot*) a *Seeker* to the *next plateau* "in sight" from the stable point already reached. There is, of course, something of a *chasm* between these points. So, it is necessary for a *Seeker* to be certain they have relieved themselves of enough "baggage" and "weight" (of *spiritual fragmentation*) in order to get enough "lift" for their ascent.

In the past, a few have even stumbled upon this point of *"crossing the abyss"* within their own traditions. But without *defragmentation*, their new-found vigor and horsepower causes them to just more quickly and deeply get lost in various distracting spiritual detours and intellectual tangents; or even fall back to old patterns, if they cannot maintain *Self-Honesty*.

This *chasm* is *not* a pitfall for *processing* mistakes—or even an *actual* barrier. But it is a "drop-off" point that many *perceive* upon reaching this part of their journey. It is sometimes enough to keep a *Seeker* from going further on the *Pathway*, fearing that they risk their existing gains. Therefore, we held off presenting the *upper-levels* until our presentation/communication of the *Pathway* had been perfected—and *Seekers* could approach this material with greater *certainty* and *ability-to-confront* its *reality*.

An *advanced Seeker* is likely to spend many months, and over *100 pro-cessing-hours*, on *Systemology Level-7*.

The *four* manuals—"*The Secret of Universes*," "*Games, Goals & Purposes*," "*The Jewel of Knowledge*" and "*Implanted Universes*"—should be treated as a single "unit" of uninterrupted work. This doesn't mean handling it as a single *session*—nor are all *Seekers* in a position to take a *retreat* from their *lives*. But daily *restimulation*, or other distractions, can significantly affect progress at this stage. Completing *Level-7* may require longer and more frequent *sessions* to achieve the same steady gains that one is previously used to.

Systemology Level-7 concerns primarily "*Games*"—which is also to say "*Universes*." On the *Standard Model*, "*Games and Universes*" is plotted at "6.0"—subordinate to the "*Alpha Thought*" ("7.0") required to *postulate* or *create* the "*Game/*

Universe" into existence. This is senior to *"Intention"* at "5.0" —which is, of course, dependent upon some *"game-condition"* for any other *consideration* to occur. [This full description provides a perspective for just what *"upper-level"* part of the *Pathway* we are now treating with *Systemology Level-7*.]

Advanced Manuals should be studied in the sequential order in which they are numbered.

Review these prerequisite materials first:
PC Lesson-7, "Eliminating Barriers"
PC Lesson-8, "Conquest of Illusion"
PC Lesson-11, "Spiritual Implants"
PC Lesson-12, "Games & Universes"
PC Lesson-14, "Spiritual Machinery"
PC Lesson-15, "The Arcs of Infinity"
AT Manual #1, "The Secret of Universes"
AT Manual #2, "Games, Goals & Purposes"
AT Manual #3, "The Jewel of Knowledge"

A.T. MANUAL #4
IMPLANTED
UNIVERSES

PIERCING THE SEVENTH VEIL

The descent of the *Alpha-Spirit* into entrapment within *this Physical Universe* has been a very long journey—through many *existences*; many *Universes*. This is reflected in the data found in all three prior *Systemology Level-7 AT Manuals*, starting with *"The Secret of Universes."* [A *Seeker* should review this material before proceeding with the current manual.]

The Way Out is also a long journey—*but possible.*

Among past attempts and other avenues available to a *Seeker*: targeting *"magical powers"* or emphasizing *"spiritual (or psychic) abilities"* directly has not led to a *Way Out*. In fact, these *"powers,"* when handled by *fragmented individuals*, only lead to more *problems*—and the *"abilities,"* themselves, fall away again, lost and forgotten. This is because we have a bad habit of *"Not-Knowing"* for (supposedly) *"one's own good."*

At the completion of *Systemology Level-7*, we are fast approaching a vast terrain of *upper-level work* to continue our progress on the *Pathway*. This, itself, has already required many years of research, and collaborative efforts of many *advanced Seekers*. The *upper-most routes* of the *Pathway* will continue to require additional research by *serious practitioners*.

Up until now, previous *processing-levels* (including *Level-7*), have all followed a "straight-shot" up the *Pathway* toward *Ascension*. In this manual, we begin treating some elements more experimentally —as it is the result of more recent *"upper-level research processing,"* rather than what is presented for *Levels 0 to 7*, which were in constant development for decades prior to publication.

While our "formal" *Advanced Training* may end with the forthcoming manuals representing *Systemology Level-8* (and completing the *"Keys to the Kingdom"* series), this will also open up, what is referred to by the *Mardukite Academy* as, the *"Infinity Grade."* This means that there remains to be plenty of room for many more researchers to contribute; but only after first completing their *Training* regarding the parts of our *"Map"* that *is* already researched, well-plotted, effective in application, and thus published.

The basic foundation of all our *fragmentation* originates from a time when the *Alpha-Spirit* still operated *knowingly* from a *godlike* state—still *knowingly capable* of *creating* and *destroying* "Universes" at will. Although our potential remains, the *realization* and *actualization* of this state has since greatly decayed.

A *godlike being* first becomes *fragmented*, then consequently loses their *"power."* AT

Manual #1 describes an early period of *clarity* and *power,* followed by a period of greatly *fragmented activity* (but still while the *Alpha-Spirit* wields its *godlike power*).

Prior to entrapment to more *solidly fixed reality-agreements* and *Bodies,* the *Alpha-Spirit* has no *considerations* (no *postulates*) in place to provide a *reality* of any *actual* harm. So, when such *powerful beings* came into great *conflict* with each other, there was really very little one could do to even *affect* another. All that one had at their disposal was trickery, false data, and misdirection—and of course, this was still a time when *Universes* were easily made...

BEFORE BETA-EXISTENCE

Implanted Universes (sometimes referred to in previous manuals as *"Penalty Univ-*

erses") were designed specifically and intentionally to *fragment* an *Alpha-Spirit*.

The earliest *"Implanted Penalty Universes"* appear in the *"Home Universe"* era. These *constructs* *"implanted"* (or *"installed"*) a *tendency* to *create* certain styles and types of *"form."* Although there are certainly variations in *creations* and *forms*, the basic *patterns* and *preferences* stemming from this early period have continued in our experience of other large *Shared Universes* (*Beta-Existences*)—including *this Physical Universe*.

In *Systemology*, a *"Universe"* is defined as: a self-contained *system* (or *package*) of *reality-agreements* (*"rules"*) and *creations* (*"objects,"* &tc.)—requiring some kind of *Space* (in which to keep *creations* separate) and some kind of *Time* (in order to observe changes in *objects* or *conditions* and the *sequencing of events*). *Systematically,* *"Universes"* are:

CREATED	by *postulate/Alpha-Thought*; with *reality-agreements*; *consideration* of the *IS-factor*.
SUSTAINED/ PERPETUATED	by *changes* in *space-time*; the *participation* in *alteration* of the *IS-factor*.
MADE SOLID	by *individuals* in *agreement* sharing *reality*.

Although it may seem like an *over-simplification* (or even ridiculous to a casual uninitiated reader), the fact remains that:

An Alpha-Spirit shifts between Universes by shifting reality-agreements.

This is still very much the case today. The major complication (or *real* challenge) in this, that we have found, is not the "*getting into*" a different *Universe* part; it is the "*getting out*" from under the accumulated weight of *fragmented considerations* regarding a *present one*.

The *reality-agreements* with *this Physical Universe* are very "heavy" and "sticky." Even at *Level-7*, a *Seeker* might easily connect with another *Universe* by contacting a *Being*—or simply *creating a Beingness*—there and "getting into agreement" with them. But the sense of *reality* is still going to be quite "vague" so long as the individual is still heavily *restrained here*, or *unwilling* to fully "*let go*" of *reality-agreements* and *attachments* to their *Earth-life*.

During the "*Home Universe*" era there were *agreed-upon Universes* for "common interaction" among *Beings*; and, of course, there were *non-agreed upon "Personal 'Home' Universes"* subject to the individual themselves. But, there were no "*solidly*" *agreed-upon Universes*—meaning none which an *Alpha-Spirit* couldn't "*get out*" of.

Shifting between *Universes*, at that time, was quite simply a matter of *intention* (or *selective agreement*)—such as how we might consider the *decision* to "*open and walk through a door*" before actually *doing* it.

Our knowledge of the "*Home Universe Matrix*" demonstrates that not all *Universes* experienced on the *Backtrack* have been large *Shared Universes*, of the type that we inhabit in common with many other *Alpha-Spirits*. These larger *Shared Universe systems*—such as *this Physical Universe* and the *Magic Universe* preceding it—are what we highlight the most in *AT Manual #1*, "*The Secret of Universes*." But, a *Seeker* may also notice references to many others, including "*Pocket Universes*" and eventually "*Penalty Universes*."

To understand this early era, we might *consider* what is of actual *value* to a *godlike Alpha-Spirit*—and that is *creation* and one's own *creations*. There is an "*interest*" inherently attached to *novelty* (*newness*) and *aesthetic* qualities (of *beauty, &tc.*) that are possible to experience with someone else's *creation*. There is also a *tendency* to desire *validation* and *admiration* (or essentially *"agreement"*) from others towards one's own *creations* in order to make them more *vivid*, *solid* and/or *"real."*

Alpha-Spirits began *creating* to "show off" their *creations* to others as a form of entertainment. This *upper-level* of *creation* did not concern simple *"objects"* or *"constructs,"* like how one might *build*, *film*, *paint* or *write* something today (although the intended purpose was the same). Rather, one would *create* an entire *"Pocket-Universe"* (small *sealed-system*) in which to "display" their *creation* as a complete *"immersive-artform"* experience. It did not take very long for this to become a *"competitive"* activity.

These *"Storytelling Pocket Universes"* allowed an individual to essentially *"live out"* the *role* of a *"movie-persona"* as a full *three-dimensional* (3-D) *holographic illusion*, rather than simply "looking at" or "watching" something. However, similar to modern *film*, these were each a separate *Universe* in their own right—and followed a separate *track* of perceived *Time* that ran a "program" or "script" from *beginning* to *end*.

An individual would simply get *"in agreement"* with the *Universe* in order to access it (*shift their Awareness*) and have the *start* of *script* flick "on." If you *consider* a *multi-plex movie theatre* today: you get in *agreement* with one of the many *"Theatre Universes"* that you *decide* to experience as *reality*—and the others are just as equally *real*, but in a completely separate *Space-Time* than yours.

Of course, when one *considers* such *creations*: there is relatively little *"freedom"* or *"choice"* involved with the *"scripted"* events and elements—much like a prerecorded *"tape"* or *"video."* In theory, one might be able to *"Play," "Stop,"* or *"Rewind"*—but the actual *internal struct-*

ure of the *creation* is not able to be changed from within it. To do that, much like today, you would essentially have to *copy* the whole thing (while *exterior to* it) in order to *edit* (*remove*), *rearrange elements*, and/or *add* something, and basically *recreate* it.

IMPLANTING UNIVERSES

"Pocket Universes" were an early precursor to what would become the *"Penalty Universes."* We have covered the *"Creation of Universes"* and even *"Infinity Exercises"* in previous manuals and the *PC-Lessons*. From this material it is easy to understand that as an alternative to *creating* each and every *facet* and *detail* of a *Universe*, one can *create/postulate* an *"Infinity"* as an *Alpha-Thought*.

In many ways, this *"Infinity"* is what we see represented by modern *"fractal geom-*

etry" and other similar progressions of a *repetitive pattern*—no matter how complex. These *patterns* can be *created/postulated "out to 'Infinity',"* as a simple *consideration* of *Alpha-Thought.* Our present *Physical Universe* contains a *creative-postulate* of *"infinite space"*—but there are other ways in which such *Space* could *manifest.*

For example: a *Universe* based on an *"infinite postulate"* of *"Mud"* would result in an *existence* purely of *"Mud"* extending *out to Infinity*; and it would only get *"thicker"* and *"blacker"* the deeper/further you *"dug in to"* it. And if you were to wonder, *"well, what's on the 'other side' of all that Mud?"*—well, there *isn't* an *"other side"* postulated for that *existence.* But, if that were the *"postulate"* for a *Universe*, it would be the *primary postulate* to *defragment "As-It-Is"* in order to be *free* of it. The purpose of this specific example may or may not be apparent to the *Seeker* at this present time.

Some of our most basic foundations for *spiritual fragmentation* occur during the *Home Universe* era. An *Alpha-Spirit* spent a lot of "*time*" in the *creation* (and *preferential perfection*) of their own *Home Universe*. By this point of the *Backtrack*, there is a tendency forming to *not want* to "*let go*" of *creations*. But, unfortunately this is what allowed an *Alpha-Spirit* to be *trapped* by them. [Ref: *AT Manual #1; collapse* of the *Home Universe Matrix* into a single *agreed-upon Universe.*]

Since *Universes* are *entered-by-agreement*, it is possible to *enforce* a *set* (or *package*) of *reality-agreements* and *cause* (*force*) an *Alpha-Spirit* to *shift Universes*. An example of this would be to *enforce* an *agreement* with the *entry-point* of the *track* for a *Pocket-Universe*. This causes one to experience the whole "*recording.*" And a *Pocket-Universe* could theoretically even *enforce* yet another *set* of *reality-agreements*, *&tc.*

Universe-shifting Incidents are "between-points" that some perceive as being at the *start* of a *track* for a *Universe*. To use our most familiar example: *Implanting-Incident #1* for *this Physical Universe* is what we treat as the *Entry-Incident* in previous material. The "*False Jewel*" and "*Heaven Implant*" take place within their own *Pocket Universes* as the "transition" from the *Magic Universe* to *this Physical Universe*.

These *Incidents* are sometimes challenging to properly *confront* on the *Backtrack*, because an individual can possibly find an *earlier Incident #1* (earlier time on the *Backtrack* that *Incident #1* occurred), they both will *register* on a *Biofeedback Device* as being "*the start of time*." Such an *Incident* will always occur at "*the start of time*" for that *track*.

In our familiar example: *Implant Platforms* of the "*False Jewel*" lead to another *Pocket-Universe* for the "*Heaven Implant*." Both of these *parts* occur prior to experiencing the *Space-Time* of *this Physical Universe*. The

"*Heaven*" part of the *Incident* ends with "*waves of blackness*" as the "*infinite postulate.*" From that point onward, no other changes occur. *Attention* turns "inward" and it leaves an *Alpha-Spirit* to *consider* the *reality-agreements* (just *installed*), which result in eventually *shifting* fully "*here*" to *this Beta-Existence.*

Consider if *Alpha-Spirits* had once divided up into teams for *games*—and each team was responsible for *creating* a *fragmented* "*Penalty Universe*" (a *Universe* promoting *fragmentation*) that could be used on the "losers." The *reality-agreement*, in this case, would consist of "winning" teams *ganging up* on "losing" teams— then "*blanketing*" individuals and *pushing them in* to the *Penalty Universe.*

Regardless of how "*horrific*" such *Penalty Universes* were, at first they would have been only mildly effective—or *distasteful* —to a *godlike being.* And regardless of who first *won*, everyone would have kept playing at this and getting *pushed through* more and more of the *Penalty Universes.*

Early on, any *"kickback"* from the *"harmful-acts"* (of *pushing others in*) would have been quite mild; but they, too, would have contributed to our *spiritual degradation.* The *"kickback"* from actually experiencing a *Penalty Universe* would result from the *fragmented considerations, postulates* and *decisions* that an individual made as a result of the experience. This progressively affected the original native *"horsepower"* of our *Alpha-Thought.*

The original *Penalty Universes* were not intended as permanent *"prisons."* Such things came later. These original ones were intended to be quite temporary— simply placing an individual in a specific situation where they would have to make *fragmented decisions* in order to escape it. The tendency toward declining states of *Beta-Awareness* (*misemotion, &tc.*) would have been *installed* in this wise.

Fixed patterns and *systems* of *this Physical Universe* appear repeatedly in the *Implants* of previous *Universes*. The original native *Alpha* state is void of all *patterns* or *systems*; these are all *created* (and later *agreed-upon*) as a result of *fragmentation*. These are what we handle as *archetypal "items"* (*command-postulates* or *objects*), while *defragmenting* the *Implant-Platforms*.

The *Spheres of Existence* and *Arcs of Infinity*, what is represented by the *Beta-Awareness Scale* and *Standard Model*—all of these are *Systems*, meaning *fixed patterns*; meaning also *fragmented patterns*. In them we find the structure of our *reality-agreements*, our *considerations*, our *impulses* and *tendencies*, and our *reactivity* and *automated machinery*. All of these are the product of an individual's own *Alpha-Thought*, however *fragmented* it may have become.

Although the same *symbolism* is often used for restimulation, we do not find direct experiences with *Penalty Universes* on the *Backtrack* of *this Physical Universe*. By this point of *condensation*, the *reality-agreements* of *Alpha-Spirits* are more *fixedly* "*stuck*" in *this Universe*. Other than the *Entry-Incident*, all of the *Implanting* taking place *within this Physical Universe* is actually more "*technological*" or "*electronic*" in nature.

To be *systematic* and *effective*: we must distinguish the "*Implanted Universe*" *symbols* and *items* (that reappear in later *Implants*), from the original "*Implanted Penalty Universes*" themselves.

For example: the "*To Eat*" *Implant-Goal* (which is part of the "*Tiger Goals*" series) originates in the original "*Tiger Penalty Universe.*" The same *items* and *symbols* also appear in later (more recent) "*electronic*" *Implants*. However, in the original *incidents*, one is *imprinted* with the experience of really *being a tiger*—and the experience of *eating* things. Whereas, in the later *electronic incidents*, only *imagery* or *pictures* of "tigers" are used in the *Implant,* along with the accompanying *command-items.* This *restimulates* "charge" from the *imprinting* of an original *Implanted Penalty Universe,* and thereby making the "*electronic*" *Implants* more significant.

IMPLANTED PENALTY UNIVERSES

If we are to be absolutely technical: full handling of this manual is a *Systemology Level-8* endeavor. But, as we complete our *Level-7* "*unit*" pertaining to *Games, Implants,* and *Universes,* this manual is an appropriate "transition point" to the upper-most reaches of the *Pathway.* For the time being: a *Seeker* may personally *consider* this material as "speculative" until a greater personal *reality* of it unfolds. In brief: don't let the study and use of *this* manual hold up moving forward to *Level-8.*

Systematic processing for *running "Implanted Penalty Universes"* (and their *symbols/items*) requires a lot of *"Spotting"* — which is to say, the *perception* and *realization* of *"What-IS"* — noticing *"What-IS"* there in the *incidents.*

At these *upper-levels* of handling *Implants:* we are primarily *defragmenting-by-Awareness;* which is to say *targeted attention* or *analytical inspection.* But in order to *defragment* in this way, we must first have a *"clear view"* of an *incident, "As-It-Is."*

An important part of *processing-out turbulent fragmentation* and *fixed considerations* from the *Backtrack* is targeting (*spotting*) the *Harmful-Acts* connected to, or associated with, *Implanting-Incidents.* By this, we do not only mean those efforts *against you by others,* but also your own efforts *against others.* Focus on any areas of "significant regret" that might *resurface*; its *imprinting* often remains as a *"still"* image or *impression*.

The original *Implanted Penalty Universes* set up the basis for our later *spiritual fragmentation* to take place. All *fragmentation* accumulates on some *"platform"* or "foundation" in order to exist. Without such deeply *Implanted/installed* "*items*" in place, there would be no *fragmentation.* By definition, something must *be there* to *fragment.*

By the point of the *Home Universe* era, an *Alpha-Spirit's* fragmented agreements mainly only consisted of a *preference* for 3-D *constructs* and *perceptions*, along with the *preference* to establish a *Home Universe* in connection to a "*matrix*" that allowed for *communication* with others and mutual "displaying" of *creations* for entertainment.

During that era, an *Alpha-Spirit* is still

quite *godlike* and *knowingly* "indestructible" as a *Being*. There are no *fragmented considerations* concerning the (false) "necessity" of *personal survival* yet. So, while still quite capable *"creative" Beings*: the first points of *fragmentation* occur in relation to one's *investment* and personal *attachment* to their *"Home Universe"* —and the refusal to *"let go"* of their own *creations*, and those of *others*, when the *Home Universe Matrix* "collapsed."

The *8 Spheres of Existence* and *8 Arcs of Infinity* provide data for *16 dynamic systems*. Note that: the *Implanted Penalty Universes* —or "IPU" for future abbreviation in this manual—are not *based on* the *16 dynamic systems*. On the contrary, the *codification* of *dynamic systems* is *based on* our observation of *Implanted "patterns."* The IPU-*patterns* actually *installed* the *dynamic systems* we now recognize, where before, there weren't any. So, in the end: we *do* have a *systematic* and *practical* means of "cross-

referencing" IPU with the *16 dynamic systems.*

```
  16  dynamic systems
      each installed by
x  4  penalty universes
      equals a total of
  64  original IPU
```

The IPU are *four-dimensional constructs* of their own 3-D *Space-Time*. They each have a *fixed track* resulting in a very specific experience related to a single *"Goal."* The experience is intended to *fragment* the Goal.

An individual is *Implanted* to focus *attention* on a basic *Goal*—generally with a "positive" characteristic at the *start* or *top* —and then experience its decline or decay as they descend through *thousands* of *"items"* resulting in a *fragmented energetic-mass* of *turbulent problems* identified with the *Goal*. It is *fragmented* into a *dynamic system* of *compulsive survival,* rather than just "some activity" a *Being* might take or leave at will.

An *Implanting-Incident* generally consists of certain types of *"thought-waves"* — or else *"wave-ridges"* or *"standing-waves"* that an *Alpha-Spirit* "passes through" during the experience. Embedded within these *waves* are the *"items"* — *commands* and *objects* — that are *perceived* as part of the *incident*. [In more "modern" or "recent" *Implanting-Incidents*, these *"waves"* are transmitted *electronically*.]

The *"Implant Items"* themselves are simply *"strong suggestions"* that direct one's *attention* toward whatever an individual is intended to be "thinking" about. It is only then that subsequent experience of that *Universe-track* cause a *fragmented charge* to develop on that channel.

Technically speaking, the *Implants* themselves have relatively little "power" — simply *suggesting* or *installing* various *obsessions*, *compulsions*, *fixations*, *tendencies* and *preferences*. *Real power* remains with the individual — but these various forms of subtle *fragmentation* also *fragment* one's own clear use of *Alpha-Thought*. It is actually the *postulates*, *decisions*, and *considerations* an individual makes, themselves, as a result of *fragmented experiences*, that really cause them the most ongoing trouble in the long run.

At the *top* or *start* of the *incident* for an IPU-*Goal*, the experience is actually quite pleasant in order to draw the individual further into the IPU. The *aesthetic display* is actually quite amazing by relative comparison to the "dimness" of *this Physical Universe*—and was *created* quite brilliantly during an era of *high-power beings*. The IPU have no specific opposition terminals. The entire *Pocket-Universe* is engineered to eventually be "against you."

IPU DEFRAGMENTATION

Accessing (or *contacting*) the *incidents* requires *"Spotting"* the *high-level "aesthetic"*
quality that occurs at the *"top of the chain"*
(or *"start of the track"*). However, it is important not to get too enamored (*fascin-
ated*) by these displays (which is part of
how it became a *Spirit-Trap* in the first
place). The basic "map" of each IPU-*incident* is simply the decline of *Awareness*
(as a scale)—the progressive deterioration of conditions—from the ultimate
"sublime" down to the most "infernal
hell" states for each *Goal*.

At the *start/top* of every IPU is a brief
Entry-Incident. It provides the impression
(falsely) of the *Alpha-Spirit* freshly separating from *"Infinity"* as *"the beginning of
time"* (but of course it is only the *start* of
the *track* for *that* IPU). This begins a long
"chain" of *Implanted false data*.

The first *"item"* of every IPU *installs* the *concept* that *"To {Goal}"* is the individual's "native state." [Note that these *Implants* are *"To {Goal}"* rather than *"To Be {a Terminal}."*] This gives the *impression* that this *Goal* is the original *Alpha-Thought* before *All Space-Time,* and that it is the *reason* or *purpose* for the *Alpha-Spirit* separating as a *Being.*

For *systematic processing* purposes: the actual/earlier *beginning* of the *incident* is not *"interior to"* the IPU at all. It really begins while occupying the *"exterior" Universe,* where one was then *pushed in to* the IPU. Total *defragmentation* really requires *"Spotting"* all *"circuits"* of experience connected to incidents for each IPU. This means: Circuit-1, *"ourselves to others"* (as *Harmful-Acts*); Circuit-2, *"others to ourselves"* (where we are the victim); and even Circuit-3, the observation of *"others with others."*

IPU-handling requires a different *system-*

atic procedure than what is given in previous *AT Manuals.* All of the *Parts* for the full procedure are given below—however, only *IPU-Platforms #1* and *#2* are given in this manual.

Running a light "pass" of *processing* on each IPU using only the beginning of this procedure is the preferred way to enter into this area of work. This will *disperse* or *discharge* the more *turbulent* (*heavier*) and *accessible* "*fragmented charge*" before treating each individual IPU any further. A *Seeker* will be able to revisit this manual at various points of *Level-8* (and thereafter), so there is no reason to "grind" hard on this now.

The basic intention at this time is simply to disperse enough "*charge*" off the original IPU-*incidents* so that it is easier to *defragment* later (more recent) *Implants* and *imprinting,* which restimulate these antiquated IPU "*dramatizations*" in our "present-time" *thoughts* and *behavior.*

STANDARD PROCEDURE:
IPU INCIDENTS

0. ENTRY: The *Alpha-Spirit* is blanketed by another and *pushed in to* the *incident*.

1. IPU-PLATFORM #1: *"The False Jewel"* (an *Implant-pattern* that is common to all IPU). [Different from *"The Jewel"* treated for *this Physical Universe* (in *AT Manual #3*), but designed with the same purpose.]

2. IPU-PLATFORM #2: *"The Symbols."* To have any significance to an individual during the IPU experience, the *object-item* *"symbols"* for the *incident* are defined (assigned meaning) with "graphic" displays.

3. UNIVERSE ANCHORS: *"To {Goal} Is To Look For ___."* The individual is directed to *spot* various things, extending their *attention/Awareness* "out" to connect with various *"objects."* Usually paired with *"To {Goal} Is To Connect To {same object}."* This activity/step *creates* the *perception* of *Space*

in which to personally experience the IPU. [This is the formation of *universal anchor-points* between the individual and the IPU.]

4. AGREEMENTS: "*To {Goal} Is To Agree To The ___.*"; "*To {Goal} Is For The ___ To Become Real.*" At the *top* of the "*chain*" this *Part* is met with great expectation and anticipation. Later on, toward the *bottom* of this *incident,* the individual meets this part with dread (even paralyzing fear) over what new nightmare will present itself.

5. FRAGMENTED MEMORY: "*To {Goal} Is To Remember Agreeing To (a) Before (b) .*" The *items* from *Part-4* (above) are repeated, but in a different order. This *impresses* us to *remember* things *out-of-sequence.*

6. THE CONFUSION: The individual becomes confused about the *sequence* of *agreements* leading up to this *Part.*

7. FUTURE POSTULATE: "*To {Goal} Is To*

Have Future {item}." The *items/symbols*
representing *reality-agreements* are
extended into the *future*. Usually paired
with *"To {Goal} Is To Predict {item} In Your
Future."* The *impressions* are really
nonsense, but it gets the individual
interested that "something is *going to*
happen" in the IPU.

8. DECISIONS: An individual's personal
decisions; usually about wanting to just
get through quickly to the end of this
lengthy *incident* and *connect* with a
"terminal" (Body).

9. JOINING: *Implant-items* about *deciding*
to get *into* a *"terminal" (Body)*.

10. THE IPU: The *Alpha-Spirit "being as"*
an individual *"terminal" (Body)*
experiencing a *real "Pocket-Universe."* The
beginning of this part of the *track* is
always a series of 7 experiences of the
Goal, starting with the "sublime" top-
level and then descending downscale.

The best sequence for working through each IPU is: from "CREATE" down to "ENDURE." Initially, a *Seeker* will only make a "light pass" through each IPU, using only *IPU-Platform #1*.

It is quite possible that a *Seeker* will only get a single *GSR-Meter* "*read*" on each *item*, or possibly every other *item*. A "*read*" might occur only on the *description*, or the *item*, or *both*. After a few passes through all *64 IPU* (handling each individually), a *Seeker* may then apply *IPU-Platform #2* (immediately following an application of *IPU-Platform #1*), and even start "*Spotting*" other *Parts* (listed above) of the *incident* (and take "*charge*" off of those).

When this is treated at *Level-8*, a *Seeker* might also "Spot" the *restimulative* use of IPU-*Symbolism* in more recent *Implanting-Incidents* taking place on the *Backtrack within this Physical Universe*. There is also the matter of handling *Entities* and *Ident-*

ity-Fragments on more progressive passes through this manual later on.

Here, we are most concerned with *defragmenting* whatever is accessible at one's current "level." *Upper-level Systemology* is not so clearly "*graded*" as what we find earlier on the *Pathway*—so, a *Seeker* keeps working at various *processes*, *defragmenting* what is *accessibly* there, and uncovering new *layers* to *defragment.*

The "*This Means...*" *items* from *IPU-Platform* #2 (such as the "*Time*" representation, *&tc.*) will lead to other "*content*" about the IPU that can be "*Spotted.*" A *Seeker* can keep records concerning any additional details that are perceived. [While some experimental use of *IPU-Platform #1* has proven effective without a *GSR-Meter*, any type of additional "*research processing*" (to directly uncover unpublished details) really requires a *Biofeedback Device* to be *systematic.*]

Advisement: When handling IPU, always *end-session* with the "top" of *IPU-Platform #1*—*Spotting* the first *item* (about "*Native State*") and making sure its *defragmentation* is stable (not giving *Meter-reads*). The same action is used as the "*key destimulator*" for this procedure—*Spotting* the *top* of *IPU-Platform #1*, if suddenly finding too much *turbulence* to *confront* while *IPU-processing*.

Note: "*To Survive*" is *not* actually one of the *64* IPU-*Goals*; it is embedded as an underlying concept within all of them. Each defines a basic *Goal* and then *impresses* its use in the effect of "*To Be {Goal}-ing Is To Survive.*" This is more "solidly" evident in the lower *dynamic systems* (meaning the *8 Spheres of Existence*).

The *IPU-List* is below. Each of the *16 dynamic systems* (whether *Arcs of Infinity* or *Spheres of Existence*) are assigned 4 IPU. Each of the *64* total IPU are distinguished by the basic *Goal* and a common *terminal* (as a *Body Type*). None of the IPU were *Implanted* in "*English*" (or any human speech), so semantic approximations given below (and in the IPU-*Directory*) may differ slightly for some *Seekers*.

16. **CREATION** (*Arc 8*)

  1. "TO CREATE"   {*statue*}
  2. "TO CAUSE"   {*old man god*}
  3. "TO DUPLICATE"   {*computer*}
  4. "TO IMAGINE"   {*cartoon*}

15. **KNOWINGNESS** (*Arc 7*)

  5. "TO KNOW"   {*2-headed dodo*}
  6. "TO UNDERSTAND" {*chipmuck*}
  7. "TO ABSORB"   {*epic hero*}
  8. "TO LEARN"   {*gnome*}

14. **GAMES** (*Arc 6*)

  9. "TO PLAY"   {*child*}
  10. "TO COMPETE"   {*coach*}
  11. "TO MANIPULATE" {*penguin banker*}

12. "TO EXCHANGE" {*spirit-broker*}

13. CHANGE (*Arc 5*)

13. "TO SHAPE" {*clay people*}

14. "TO CHANGE" {*magician*}

15. "TO COMBINE" {*conjoined twins*}

16. "TO (BRING) ORDER" {*gorilla people*}

12. REASON (*Arc 4*)

17. "TO REASON" {*clown*}

18. "TO ORIENT" {*wire man*}

19. "TO GUIDE" {*pilot*}

20. "TO COMPUTE" {*toy bodies*}

11. CONSTRUCTION (*Arc 3*)

21. "TO CONSTRUCT" {*beavers*}

22. "TO ARRANGE" {*blockhead*}

23. "TO BUILD" {*snake people*}

24. "TO STRUCTURE" {*crystals*}

10. AESTHETICS (*Arc 2*)

25. "TO INVENT" {*dwarves*}

26. "TO ENHANCE" {*ghost people*}

27. "TO INSPIRE"   {muses}

28. "TO BEAUTIFY"   {fairy godmother}

9. ETHICS (Arc 1)

29. "TO PURIFY"   {fire people}

30. "TO JUDGE"   {minotaur}

31. "TO DEFEND"   {little green men}

32. "TO STRENGTHEN"   {energy ball}

8. DIVINITY (Sphere 8)

33. "TO ENLIGHTEN"   {rabbit preacher}

34. "TO CONVERT"   {fish man}

35. "TO COMMUNE"   {feminine angel}

36. "TO WORSHIP"   {holy knights}

7. SPIRITS (Sphere 7)

37. "TO PREDICT"   {soothsayer}

38. "TO INFLUENCE"   {cupid/cherub}

39. "TO COLLECT"   {elves/fairies}

40. "TO EMBODY"   {satyr}

6. UNIVERSE (Sphere 6)

41. "TO DISCOVER"   {centaurs}

42. "TO LOCATE"   {leprechaun}

43. "TO GATHER"   {spacesuit body}

44. "TO OWN"   {fox people}

5. <u>LIFEFORMS</u> (Sphere 5)

45. "TO GROW"   {genetic entity}

46. "TO LIVE"   {dinosaur}

47. "TO HEAL"   {tree man}

48. "TO ADAPT"   {thread man}

4. <u>SOCIETY</u> (Sphere 4)

49. "TO ESTABLISH"   {3-eyed giants}

50. "TO SHARE"   {dolphins}

51. "TO CONTROL"   {frog king}

52. "TO UNITE"   {dog soldiers}

3. <u>GROUPS</u> (Sphere 3)

53. "TO ORGANIZE"   {file clerk}

54. "TO COOPERATE"   {robots}

55. "TO PARTICIPATE"   {merfolk}

56. "TO EXPAND"   {railroad engineer}

2. <u>HOME</u> (Sphere 2)

57. "TO JOIN"   {cat people}

58. "TO REPRODUCE" {*insect invader*}

59. "TO SATISFY"   {*cavemen*}

60. "TO CARE (FOR)" {*bird girl*}

1. **SELF/BODY** (*Sphere 1*)

61. "TO EXPERIENCE" {*bear*}

62. "TO REPLENISH" {*a Sumerian*}

63. "TO EAT"   {*tiger*}

64. "TO ENDURE"   {*pyramid*}

IPU-PLATFORM # 1

IPU-Platform #1 is the "*False Jewel*" *Entry-Incident* for the original IPU. By this point, a *Seeker* should already be familiar with *running* these "*Implant-Platforms*" as a *systematic defragmentation process*. [Refer to: *PC-11 & 12; AT #1, #2 & #3.* That material will not be repeated here.]

The "*IPU Jewel*" is a *seven-dimensional construct* with a *diamond-like structure*.

When viewed with 3-D *perception*: this *False Jewel* appears very much like *two 4-sided pyramids* sharing a common base. There is, however, a *sense* that it extends into *spaces beyond* 3-D *perception*. [Its complete *form* has *64 x 2 (128) facets* or *sides*, but only a few are actually perceived during an IPU-*incident*.]

IPU-Platform #1 "command-items" are *spotted* along with *The Jewel* (*construct*) itself. The *items* mainly appear in groups of *three* (*e.g.*, X.1, X.2, X.3), which correspond to the *three* possible *positions* of *The Jewel* during the *incident*: (1) on the *left side*; (2) on the *right side*; and (3) in *front-center*.

There are also three possible *conditions* of *The Jewel* that correspond to the *positions*: (1) *Jewel* begins to appear; (2) *Jewel* becomes more substantial; (3) *Jewel* flashes (with the *item end-word*) and disappears. Memorize the pattern below; these instructions will not be added to the *Processing Command Lines* (PCL), nor will

"Spot the Alpha" (see *AT Manual #3*)—although all of this will still be implied for the procedure.

1.X.1   *Jewel* begins to *appear* on the *left side.*

1.X.2   *Jewel* becomes *more substantial* on the *right side.*

1.X.3   *Jewel* is *front* and *center, flashes* then *disappears.*

Additionally, *The Jewel* starts a certain *"distance"* away; then is *perceived* as getting *closer* with each grouped-set of three *items*—until finally it is *"touching you"* at the end of *IPU-Platform #1.*

Restimulation of the IPU-*incidents* occurs in later (more recent) *Universes* (see *AT Manual #1*). Restimulation of more recent *Implanting* may result in uncomfortable sensations (or pressure) in the forehead when *contacted* in *processing*. This is more appropriately handled in *Level-8.*

For now, a *Seeker* should focus *attention* on the original IPU—which is essentially the *earliest similar incident* on the *Backtrack.* The later (more recent) *Implanting-Incidents* can be easily distinguished from the original IPU experiences. In later uses, there are always *three Jewels* present, one in each *position*; and they *flash* for every *item*. Furthermore, at the *end-word* for each, the *three Jewels* merge together as *one Jewel* in the *center* of the "*forehead.*"

IPU-Platform #1 is a detailed short-form formula. It includes *descriptions. Positions/conditions* of *The Jewel* and directions to "*Spot the Alpha*" are not written here. The *platform* contains *86-items.* This formula is used on all *64 IPU-Goals,* each handled as its own *platform-running process.* Use the *IPU Goal-List* given previously.

  1.0.1 *Spot being blanketed, blanketing another, and others blanketing others.*

1.0.2 *Spot being pushed in, pushing someone in, and others pushing others in.*

> *There is nothing; no space, no time, no dimension...*

1.1.1 "TO {*goal*} IS NATIVE STATE."
You are aware of being the Infinity of Nothingness before all time.

1.1.2 "TO {*goal*} IS TO BE THE STATIC."
As a basic static, you want non-static; you want something to happen, for there to be something.

1.1.3 "TO {*goal*} IS THE URGE FOR SOMETHINGNESS."

You realize the urge; and it makes sense.

1.2.1 "TO BASIC URGE IS TO {*goal*}."
Making sense of the urge; you receive this impression.

1.2.2 "BEFORE THE BEGINNING, NOW, AND FOREVER, IS THE URGE, AND THE URGE IS TO {*goal*}."

You realize all other "urges" will stem from this.

1.2.3 "TO {*goal*} IS THE BASIS FOR ALL URGES."

You feel the strength of the "urge" growing.

1.3.1 "TO {*goal*} IS TO NEED RELIEF."
You realize what is needed for relief.

1.3.2 "THE BASIC RELIEF WILL COME FROM {*goal*}-ING."
You realize all "relief" stems from this.

1.3.3 "TO {*goal*} IS THE BASIS FOR ALL RELIEF."

You realize that this is the reason for everything.

1.4.1 "TO {*goal*} IS THE ORIGINAL REASON WHY."
This makes sense to you.

1.4.2 "THE BASIC REASON WHY IS THE NEED TO {*goal*}."
You realize all other "reasons" stem from this.

1.4.3 "TO {*goal*} IS THE BASIS FOR
ALL REASONS WHY."

*You realize you need to "do
something" about this.*

1.5.1 "TO {*goal*} IS TO ACT."

This makes sense to you.

1.5.2 "THE BASIC ACTION IS TO
{*goal*}."

*You realize all other "actions" stem
from this.*

1.5.3 "TO {*goal*} IS THE BASIS FOR
ALL ACTION."

*You realize you need to "decide
something" before anything will
happen.*

1.6.0 "TO {*goal*} IS TO DECIDE."

You choose to make the decision.

1.6.1 "BEFORE THE BEGINNING,
NOW, AND FOREVER, IS THE
DECISION, AND THE DECISION
IS TO {*goal*}."

*Space becomes filled with faint
sourceless golden light. {"Spot the
Space"}*

> *You realize that {goal} is the first*
> *decision.*

1.6.2 "THE ORIGINAL DECISION IS
    TO {*goal*}."

> *You realize all other "decisions" stem*
> *from this.*

1.6.3 "TO {*goal*} IS THE BASIS FOR
    ALL DECISIONS."

> *You "postulate" that there will be*
> *something.*

1.7.1 "TO {*goal*} IS TO POSTULATE."

> *You realize that this is the first*
> *postulate.*

1.7.2 "THE BASIC POSTULATE IS
    TO {*goal*}."

> *You realize all other "postulates"*
> *stem from this.*

1.7.3 "TO {*goal*} IS THE BASIS FOR
    ALL POSTULATES."

> *You postulate time. Time exists to*
> *allow for change due to {goal}-ing.*

1.8.1 "TO {*goal*} IS THE SOURCE OF
    TIME."

You realize the basic consideration of time is past, present, and future {goal}-ing.

1.8.2 "THE BASIS OF TIME IS {goal}-ING."

You realize all future "considerations of time" will stem from this.

1.8.3 "TO {goal} IS THE BASIS OF ALL TIME."

You "agree" with the concept of {goal}-ing.

1.9.1 "TO {goal} IS TO AGREE."

You realize this is the basic agreement.

1.9.2 "THE BASIC AGREEMENT IS TO {goal}."

You realize all other agreements stem from this.

1.9.3 "TO {goal} IS THE BASIS OF ALL AGREEMENT."

You create energy formed of the concept of {goal}-ing.

1.10.1 "TO {*goal*} IS TO HAVE
ENERGY."

*You realize this is the most basic of
all energies.*

1.10.2 "THE BASIC ENERGY STEMS
FROM {*goal*}-ING."

*You realize all other energies stem
from this.*

1.10.3 "TO {*goal*} IS THE BASIS OF ALL
ENERGY."

*You postulate that {goal}-ing is the
basic reality.*

1.11.1 "TO {*goal*} IS TO REALITY."

This makes sense to you.

1.11.2 "THE BASIC REALITY IS
{*goal*}-ING."

*You realize all reality stems from
this.*

1.11.3 "TO {*goal*} IS THE BASIS OF ALL
REALITY."

*You postulate matter (mass); the
most real mass stems from {goal}.*

1.12.1 "TO {*goal*} IS TO MATTER."

You realize this is the most basic of all matter.

1.12.2 "THE BASIC MATTER STEMS FROM {*goal*}-ING."

You realize all other matter stems from this.

1.12.3 "TO {*goal*} IS THE SOURCE OF ALL MATTER."

You postulate that likingness (affinity) is achieved through {goal}-ing.

1.13.1 "TO {*goal*} IS LOVE."

This makes sense to you.

1.13.2 "THE BASIC LOVE IS ACHIEVED THROUGH {*goal*}-ING."

You realize all love stems from this.

1.13.3 "TO {*goal*} IS THE BASIS OF ALL LOVE."

You postulate that basic interchange is through {goal}-ing.

1.14.1 "TO {*goal*} IS TO COMMUNICATE."

You realize that this is the first communication.

1.14.2 "THE BASIC COMMUNICATION IS {*goal*}-ING."

You realize all communication stems from this.

1.14.3 "TO {*goal*} IS THE BASIS OF ALL COMMUNICATION."

You realize that {goal}-ing will bring understanding.

1.15.1 "TO {*goal*} IS TO REACH FOR UNDERSTANDING."

This makes sense to you.

1.15.2 "THE ATTAINMENT OF UNDERSTANDING IS THROUGH {*goal*}-ING."

You realize all understanding stems from this.

1.15.3 "TO {*goal*} IS THE BASIS OF ALL UNDERSTANDING."

You postulate space in which to {goal}.

1.16.1 "TO {*goal*} IS TO HAVE SPACE."

You realize this is what creates space.

1.16.2 "THE DELINEATION OF SPACE
IS BY {*goal*}-ING."

You realize all other spaces stem from this.

1.16.3 "TO {*goal*} IS THE BASIS OF ALL
SPACE."

You postulate that {goal}-ing gives meaning to existence.

1.17.1 "TO {*goal*} IS TO HAVE
MEANING."

This makes sense to you.

1.17.2 "THE BASIC MEANING IS IN
REGARDS TO {*goal*}-ING."

You realize all other meaning stems from this.

1.17.3 "TO {*goal*} IS THE BASIS OF ALL
MEANING."

You postulate that {goal}-ing is truth.

1.18.1 "TO {*goal*} IS TRUTH."

This makes sense to you.

1.18.2 "THE ATTAINMENT OF BASIC
TRUTH IS THROUGH
{*goal*}-ING."

You realize all other truth stems
from this.

1.18.3 "TO {*goal*} IS THE BASIS OF ALL
TRUTH."

You postulate havingness; the most
real sense of havingness is to {goal}.

1.19.1 "TO {*goal*} IS HAVE."

You realize this is the most basic of
all havingness.

1.19.2 "THE BASIC HAVINGNESS
STEMS FROM {*goal*}-ING."

You realize all other havingness
stems from this.

1.19.3 "TO {*goal*} IS THE BASIS OF ALL
HAVINGNESS."

You postulate that {goal}-ing is the
basic aesthetic.

1.20.1 "TO {*goal*} IS BEAUTY."

This makes sense to you.

1.20.2 "THE BASIC BEAUTY IS
{*goal*}-ING."

*You realize all other beauty stems
from this.*

1.20.3 "TO {*goal*} IS THE BASIS OF ALL
BEAUTY."

*You desire to connect with the
"thoughts" in the Jewel of
Knowledge.*

1.21.1 "TO {*goal*} IS TO CONNECT
WITH THOUGHT."

This makes sense to you.

1.21.2 "THE BASIC THOUGHT
CONCERNS {*goal*}-ING."

*You realize all other thought stems
from this.*

1.21.3 "TO {*goal*} IS THE BASIS OF ALL
THOUGHT."

*You realize that {goal} will influence
all existence.*

1.22.1 "TO {*goal*} IS THE HIDDEN
INFLUENCE."

This makes sense to you.

1.22.2 "THE BASIC HIDDEN
INFLUENCE IS TO {*goal*}."

You realize this underlies all other hidden influences.

1.22.3 "TO {*goal*} IS THE BASIS OF ALL HIDDEN INFLUENCES."

You postulate that the most valuable particle is that which is {goal}-ing.

1.23.1 "TO {*goal*} IS TO VALUE."

This makes sense to you.

1.23.2 "THE MOST VALUABLE PARTICLE IS GAINED THROUGH {*goal*}-ING."

You realize all other value stems from this.

1.23.3 "TO {*goal*} IS THE BASIS OF ALL VALUATION."

You realize that {goal}-ing will bring about true existence.

1.24.1 "TO {*goal*} IS TO EXIST."

You realize this is the only reason for existing.

1.24.2 "ALL EXISTENCE DEPENDS ON {*goal*}-ING."

You realize that through this you will achieve understanding of all existence.

1.24.3 "TO {*goal*} IS THE BASIS OF ALL EXISTENCE."

The Jewel is touching you, flashes, and passes into you.

You realize that The Jewel is bringing you enlightenment.

1.25.1 "TO {*goal*} IS TO GAIN ENLIGHTENMENT."

This makes sense to you.

1.25.2 "THE BASIC ENLIGHTENMENT CONCERNS {*goal*}-ING."

You realize all other enlightenment stems from this.

1.25.3 "TO {*goal*} IS THE BASIS OF ALL ENLIGHTENMENT."

The Jewel is touching you, flashes, and passes into you.

You realize that The Jewel is bringing you knowledge.

1.26.1 "TO {*goal*} IS TO KNOW."

This makes sense to you.

1.26.2 "THE BASIC KNOWLEDGE
CONCERNS {*goal*}-ING."

*You realize all other knowledge stems
from this.*

1.26.3 "TO {*goal*} IS THE BASIS OF ALL
KNOWLEDGE."

*The Jewel is touching you, flashes,
and passes into you.*

*The Jewel remains in the center of
your beingness.*
*Something begins to appear faintly
below you; you reach for it.*

1.27.1 "TO {*goal*} IS TO REACH."

*What you are reaching for is
{goal}-ing.*

1.27.2 "THE BASIC REACH IS
TOWARD {*goal*}-ING."

*You realize all other reaches stem
from this.*

1.27.3 "TO {*goal*} IS THE BASIS OF
EVERY REACH."

The Jewel flashes within you.

*As you reach, you encounter the
basic symbols; this sets up IPU-
Platform #2.*

*You realize that reaching for them
will bring understanding.*

*Looking down at the stack of symbol-
pictures, The Jewel now seems
above you.*

1.28.1 "TO {*goal*} IS TO CONTACT
SYMBOLS."

*You contact the first and most basic
symbols of all existence.*

1.28.2 "THE BASIC SYMBOLS
CONCERN {*goal*}-ING."

*You realize, as you connect to the
first symbol, that:*

1.28.3 "TO {*goal*} IS THE BASIS OF ALL
SYMBOLOGY."

*The Jewel flashes on top of you and
seems to move you into the first
picture. [IPU-Platform #2 begins.]*

IPU-PLATFORM #2

Advisement: for *Systemology-Level-8* use.

IPU-Platform #2 concerns *"Symbols."* It immediately follows the last *item* on *IPU-Platform #1*. These *Symbols* are 3-D *image-pictures* stacked up to at least *four spatial-dimensions*. They are literally *"photographic imprints,"* but stacked like a pile of pictures. The *Symbols* are specific to each IPU. They are often elaborate *moving scenes* rather than stationary *objects*.

The basic *pattern* of *IPU-Platform #2* is:

{*see a symbol*} x {*"This Means ___."*}

The basic method for *defragmentation* is to *"Spot the Symbol"* (*object-item*) and *"This Means ___"* (*command-item*) until there is no longer a *"charge"* on that association.

The first four *items* for each IPU are always: *"This Means Time"*; *"This Means*

Space"; "This Means Energy"; and "This Means Matter." There are approximately *100-items* for each IPU. Determining these *Symbols* is technically a *Level-8 research action* applied to each IPU after several passes through *IPU-Platform #1.*

During the original IPU-*incident*: all *100-symbols/items* were run one way; then they were run again in reverse order, where the color was inverted and the orientation shifted (as like a mirror reflection). As a complete *processing action*, *IPU-Platform #2* is also *run* in this wise. A *Seeker* is encouraged to construct their own *platform-worksheets* to more easily handle this data.

Ideally: a *Seeker* will take off most of the accessible IPU-fragmentation with several passes through *IPU-Platform #1*; then they will start *spotting* the IPU-*Symbols* that become accessible by applying the start of *IPU-Platform #2.* They may then compare their *data* to our existing *data* (listed in the *"IPU-Directory"*). [The totality of potential IPU-*data* for *Platform #2* has not yet been fully researched/published (*as of 2023*).]

The *Symbols* are different for each IPU. The *items* associated with them (other than the first ones, like *"Time"*; *"Motion"*; *"Space"*; *"Energy"*; and *"Mass"*) are also not consistent across all IPU. Using available data for the "TO EAT"-IPU (or *Tiger Penalty Universe*), we provide the following *"This Means"* item-list as only one example (*in descending order*):

TIME, MOTION, SPACE, ENERGY, MASS, LIKINGNESS, REALITY, COMMUNICATION, ADMIRATION, GROWTH, ADVENTURE, FOOD, EATING, FASTNESS, DIFFICULT, DISORIENTATION, DISORDER, PAIN, TORTURE, HELL, ACHIEVEMENT, FLYING, ATTACK, AVOIDANCE, CUT, TERROR, GOD, STEALTH, BLEED, TROUBLE, DEFEAT, HOPELESSNESS, WEAKNESS, FEROCIOUSNESS, NEED,

CAPTURE, SURPRISE, SENSATION, STRIKE, BEAUTY, BREAKING, DIZZYNESS, TRAP, DEGRADATION, OBLIGATION, SUCCESS, CREATION, CONTENTMENT, AGONY, RECOVERY, HOME, AMBUSH, STRENGTH, FAILURE, WORSHIP, TEAR, YOU, RUN FAST, FORCE, HIDING, DISTANCE, COMPETITION, HUNTING, CHEATING, AMUSED, BURN, DUMB, FLEE, LEAP, TRANCE, DECAY, TO LOSE, STIFF, TURMOIL, SKILL, THROW, ROAR, UPSET, REGRET, CONFUSION, SLEEPING, DANGER, MYSTERY, UNAWARE, ROT, DISABILITY, EVIL, PANIC, TIREDNESS, INJURY, FEAR, FALL, ENTRAPMENT, HOT, ELECTRICAL (ZAP), COLD, KILL, DEATH, DOOM, FIGHT, WIN, UNIVERSE, PROCEED.

IPU-DIRECTORY

This *"Directory"* includes basic data researched for each IPU. It mainly assists *research processing* for *IPU-Platform #2*, and for handling other *Parts* of *"Standard Procedure: IPU."* This *"Directory"* follows the same sequencing given in the previous IPU-*List*. [This is a functional, but incomplete, record. The totality of potential IPU-*data* is not yet available (*as of 2023*).]

There is a general description of each original IPU-*incident*. The general pattern of an IPU-*incident* is: *"7 wonderful things"* at the top/start of each *track*; things go wrong; being chased around; captured; divided against yourself (identity fragmented); set free; deciding you can't survive; dying; being trapped in a grave; dragged off; dumped in a fiery hell-like volcano and tortured; end of IPU-*track*.

[Always end IPU-*processing* by *spotting* the top *item* of *IPU-Platform #1.*]

Although the original IPU are implanted-imprints, by the era of the *Magic Kingdom Universe*, much of this material is being "dramatized" as basic *reality-agreements* and "manifested" quite *solidly*. It remains embedded in the "*archetypal imprinting*" on the "*Thought-Planes*" of *this Physical Universe*. The *fragmentation* continues to get "restimulated" by the *mass* and *technology* of modern society and its medias.

[There is also data for "*Price*" and "*Survive*" *items* that only apply to later uses of IPU-*restimulation* in more recent *Implant-Incidents*. This is relevant for *Level-8*, when handling archaic "*Mass-Implants*" (*Devices* or *Centers*)—essentially "*Pyramids*" once located on a different copy of our present Earth (one that included *Atlantis* and *Lemuria*). Those locations are also indicated.]

Trigger Warning: This material represents the very definition of a "trigger" (in regards to the *Human Condition*). It would be strange to say that this data should be safeguarded. Since it cannot be broadcast globally (to a general audience and be properly understood), it is fair to say that this knowledge is dangerous—yet, even more so when kept secret; known by a few and used as a weapon against the many. We don't know how this data was directly gleaned by others in the past; but it has already been used for personal gain —restimulating targeted interests, manipulating attentions, controlling purchasing power and popularity.

1. "TO CREATE" {*statue*}

Time—a planet circling a sun.
Space—vast plain full of cities/peoples.
Energy—blast from space shatters a
        mountain.
Mass—worlds in collision.
God—giant sun.

Worship—people bowing before statue.
Pain—energy hits statue and cracks it.
Degraded—sunbeam divides statue.
Trouble—hooded priest of sun-gods.

Incident (track)—you are god in the form of a statue, floating around, and putting out energy beams. The statue is young at the start, but resembles an "old man" by the end. The "suns" are "senior gods" that "zap" you at the end. You do 7 great wonders and the people worship you and build you temples. As you get into trouble, you dramatize the "wrath of god" on the people. In the end you are dragged off and tortured by the beings you wronged.

Pyramid (loc.)—center of *Atlantis*.

"The Price of Creation is to be blamed."
"To Survive is to depend on worship."

2. "TO CAUSE" {old man god on throne}

Time—a golden clock set in the clouds.
Space—golden crystal celestial palace.
Energy—a wave of golden light.

Mass—the golden throne.

God—you; the old man on the throne.

Trouble—devil-beings.

Incident (track)—you perform 7 incredible acts of creation. You create people; cherubs to inspire them; and angels to bring them into communion with you. When people become troublesome, you create devils to put in ethics. But the devils turn against you and make you wrong. You smite the devils; the rebel; you cast them out. You go on rampages and destroy things; finally deciding you can't tolerate being a god anymore. You throw yourself into a volcano; the devils you smote are torturing you at the end.

Pyramid (loc.)—Atlantis.

"The Price of Causation is to be the effect."

"To Survive is to depend on subservience."

3. "TO DUPLICATE" {computer}

(Alternatively: "To Mock Up")

Time—a digital display.

Space—a flat plane.

Energy—electricity.

Gods—vortex energies.

Incident (track)—you are a large computer on an empty plain. The gods create spirits that come to you and ask you to mock up things. You perform 7 wonderful "mockups" (postulating electron structures, physical laws, and making solid things) including bodies and cities for them to live in. The "mockups" become more complex and you lose control of your creations. People start asking a lot of questions you no longer know about— mostly *"Why?"*—and you invent answers and false data. Eventually the people hate you and pray to the "vortex gods" to "zap" you.

Pyramid (loc.)—Peru.

"The Price of Creative Thought is to be questioned."

"To Survive is to depend on approval from others."

4. "TO IMAGINE" {cartoon}

Time—a watch with cartoon hands.
Space—cartoon environment.
God—giant cartoon mouse god.

Incident (track)—you are a big plastic doll body resembling a cartoon-mouse. Everyone can create illusions, which become real if they can get others to believe in them. At the top/start, you do 7 wonderful illusions (which others believe in and make real). You eventually create harmful things, which go out of control. Others get bored with your creations; so you imagine more degraded things to get their interest. They become too degraded; others are disgusted and shatter your illusions. You are taken before a giant mouse-god that divides you against yourself and puts the pieces in a mausoleum. Cartoon devils drag you into your volcano-illusion; but since you can't stop believing in it, you are trapped by your own illusion.

Pyramid (loc.)—western *Lemuria.*

"The Price of Imagination is to create your own fears."

"To Survive is to depend on illusions created by others."

5. "TO KNOW" {2-headed dodo}

Time—sun swinging across a tropical sky.
Space—tropical jungle and beach.
God—totems.

Incident (track)—your two heads allow you to see the "pictures"/"ghosts" that people carry behind them (entities and symbols attached from other *Penalty-Universes* that trail behind them). You use your perception to perform 7 great deeds, such as healing and solving problems, gaining admiration and respect from the people. But your appearance is ridiculous (and you don't want to be laughed at), so you maintain power over others by misusing your hidden knowledge, even harming others by accident. You see the "evil" each carries behind them, and become terrified of others. You start suppressing others to reduce their ability to harm you; and when this is discovered, they chase, capture, and drag you to the totem gods.

Pyramid (loc.)—northern *Lemuria*.

"The Price of Knowledge is terror."
"To Survive is to depend on the not-knowingness of others."

6. "TO UNDERSTAND" {chipmunk}

Time—sun swings over brook.
Space—forest.
God—the wise owl god.
Danger—wolf.
Deceit—a 2-headed sheep.
Slyness—a fox.
Drink—penguin drinks from stream.
Confuse—one chipmunk talking to
         another.
Sensation—a female chipmunk.

Incident (track)—you are the only one who understands the different languages of the different animals. You perform 7 noble deeds involving translation, such as saving chipmunks from predators. You translate things others don't want to hear; it causes them grief; you get blamed. You understand everyone's problems but can't solve them. No matter how hard you try to explain, the wolf still eats sheep (understanding doesn't change its nature). You start to misuse your ability; conflict breaks out. You translate for the fox, and help them trick people, in exchange for their tricking a chipmunk for you (that you want to seduce). When the owl-god discovers your treachery, you are divided against yourself, &tc.

Pyramid (loc.)—Bermuda.

"The Price of Understanding is grief."
"To Survive is to depend on the sympathy of others."

7. "TO ABSORB" {*mythological hero*}

Time—a water clock.
Mass—"Mt. Olympus"
God—mythological pantheon.

Incident (track)—you can absorb knowledge and the form of anyone, including the very real and prominent embodiments of the gods. You can even appear as faces in the sky. At top/start you go through a series of 7 clearings and overcome 7 dangers or distractions. You can then become these forms at will. The gods are oppressing and abusing people, so you use your abilities to become as one of the people, and champion them against the gods. You help people gain the knowledge of the gods; this only creates strife and resentment. The people blame you; the gods are angry with you. You start impersonating the gods, and are eventually captured and taken before "Zeus" who divides you against yourself and places "black bands" on you to prevent your taking any other forms.

Pyramid (loc.)—north central *Lemuria*.

"The Price of Wisdom is to be despised."
"To Survive is to depend on gratitude from others."

8. "TO LEARN" {gnome}

Time—a clock on a wall.

Space—library complex (view of central lawn through window).

Energy—book falling off of shelf.

Mass—huge shelves filled with books.

God—university/academy dean (statue).

Confusion—a walrus-person struggling with book.

Tiredness—a gnome asleep over a book.

Sensation—a female cat-person.

Companionship—a female gnome.

Stubborn—a bear-person.

Incident (track)—data is stored in books and scrolls and data-cubes. Only advanced students access data-cubes because it blasts the data into you. You are a eyeglass-wearing gnome, an advanced student, and a teacher. You start by solving 7 complex problems for others, become liked and well respected. You start to misdirect students to keep them from surpassing you—and have sex with students (female cat-people) in exchange for grades. The students find out; drag you before the dean; he divides you against yourself. When you try to use data-cubes again, the back-flow causes your brain to explode. They bury you in a basement; eventually toss you into a furnace that leads down to the volcano-hell.

Pyramid (loc.)—center of *Atlantis*.

"The Price of Learning is confusion."
"To Survive is to depend on respect from others."

9. "TO PLAY" {*child*}

Time—shadow of a sun swinging over village.

God—serpent-god.

Home—houses on stilts over tidal flats.

Incident (track)—you are a child among many children; very few adults or parents exist. There is an impression of being a child forever. Bodies are indestructible and "Asian" or "Eastern" in appearance; young and old are the same size. You start by playing 7 glorious games; but games go downscale rather quickly, becoming mean and vicious. Adults sometimes use you for sex; which is pleasurable, but also strange, fearsome and frustrating (without climax). Games become more turbulent; eventually a child dies (which wasn't thought possible). After organizing the most terrible of games, the people take you to the temple to the serpent-god—who divides you against yourself. You age, but the adults find you loathsome and you can't play with children anymore. You die; are buried; then taken away to an undersea volcano by snakes, where you are tortured by the children you killed.

Pyramid (loc.)—Chili.

"The Price of Joyful Exuberance is perversion."

"To Survive is to depend on the games of others."

10. "TO COMPETE" {coach/team leader}

Time—digital clock on scoreboard.

Space—game-field/arena.

Energy—steel ball smashing into grandstands.

God—the referee.

Cheat—tripping an opponent.

Detestation—fan throws food at player.

Admiration—cheering crowd.

Incident (track)—you are the coach operating from a fenced-off area (guarded by some players), responsible for instructing and planning "plays" for your team in a rather complex "steel-ball" sport. Players can get smashed by the "ball" and frequently go to the dug-out for body-repairs. You execute 7 brilliant plays; the crowd cheers. Going downscale, you are more careless with players getting hurt, you find ways to cheat, and even start working against other coaches on your side. They try to demote you. You even take a group of players and attack the fenced-off area of the opposing side's coach. Then, opponents gain strength as you start fighting against your own side. Eventually, your own team takes you to the referee, who hits you with a beam that divides you against yourself; everyone ignores you during the plays and you are trampled, your body being shattered into pieces. They call a "time out" to bury the pieces in the sand; a flag with a "cross" marks the site. Enraged fans dig you up and throw you into the volcano beneath the grandstands, where the spirits of betrayed players and fans throw things at you until the track ends.

Pyramid (loc.)—Frankfort.

"The Price of Competition is losing."
"To Survive is to depend on encouragement from others."

11. "TO MANIPULATE" {penguin banker}

Time—clock on wall of a bank.
Space—an urban business district.
God—a computer.

Trouble — poor homeless bear-people.

Incident (track) — at the top/start, you make 7 incredible business deals, such as taking over companies and outsmarting other industrialists. Downscale, you become irresponsible about the side effects of these deals; people are harmed; poor homeless (bear-people) get angry, picket, then tear down your businesses. You retaliate and incite riots against competitors before being hauled into court, where a computer-god sentences you to divide against yourself. You lose business contacts; businesses go bankrupt; banks close down; and you jump out a window. Devils (in the form of the bear-people) tear you apart and throw you into a volcano.

Pyramid (loc.) — northeastern *Greenland.*

"The Price of Profit is oppression."

"To Survive is to depend on trust from others."

12. "TO EXCHANGE" {*spirit-broker*}

Time — an hour-glass (sand running

down).

Space—rolling hills, plains; fairytale
kingdom with castle.

God—demon god (statue).

Incident (track)—you are a wizard in a
magical kingdom of 'munchkins' and
'spirits'. As a 'spirit-broker', you trick
people, or do something for them, in exchange for their "soul" (a contract for
their service as a 'spirit' after death),
which are then sold to 'demons'. At the
start, you collect 7 "souls" and sell them
to 'demons' in exchange for 7 wondrous
miracles (performed by the 'demons').
This astounds people and is rewarded by
the 'king'. Downscale, you do less for
people in exchange (to keep more of the
power for yourself); and become more
paranoid and withdrawn as more people
"almost find out" what you're doing. You
get bored with the affairs of the people
and begin engaging in sex with 'spir-
it-forms' and 'demons'. The 'spirits' start
protesting their "contracts" and the 'de-

mons' get upset with enforcing them. People start to trick you (with false "contracts"); you start blasting others with an energy-rod ("wand"), and get in trouble with the king. The 'demons' drag you before the presence of a 'demon-god' (statue), who divides you against yourself. Then you're tossed into a volcano (beneath the castle) and tortured by the 'spirits' and 'demons' you had cheated.

Pyramid (loc.)—Catskills.

"The Price of Wealth is enslavement."
"To Survive is to depend on commitment from others."

13. "TO SHAPE" {clay people}

Time—clock on large clay building.
Space—clay city (earthen slabs and
        blocks); buildings look like
        upside-down pots; cracks/fissures
        in ground give off vapor.
Energy—exploding volcano.
Mass—landslide.

Trouble—the fire-people.

Home—big clay slab building.

Incident (track)—you are a body-shaper, able to reshape bodies of clay-people (and getting them to hold the new form). At the top/start, you perform 7 wonderful body-shapings, giving people strength and beauty (earning you admiration and respect). Downscale, you conceal ugliness beneath shapings of people you don't like —so that the beautification fades (does not hold) and eventually reveals the hidden shaping instead. There are many harmful-acts and mistakes; all your forms begin to destabilize. People start to blame their deformities on a plague and lose control of their forms; you also lose control of your form. Realizing you are the cause, they chase and capture you, and you are divided against yourself, *&tc.*

Pyramid (loc.)—island off *Brazil*.

"The Price of Admiration is to conform (to others opinions)."

"*To Survive is to depend on the malleability (plasticity) of others.*"

14. "TO CHANGE" {*magician-wizard*}

Time—shadow swings across palace
       dome.

Space—Arabian-Nights styled desert city.

Energy—bolt from a wand.

Mass—city-walls falling down.

Trouble—genies (djinn).

Incident (track)—you are a wizard with the ability to 'metamorphize' into many shapes; each pass through the incident, the skin of your humanoid form is of a different color (starting with purple). Using 'spells', you start by changing into 7 wondrous forms—a winged horse, snake, mouse, gnome, &tc. You gain great power and admiration; dueling with other wizards and winning. Downscale, you abuse/misuse power, become arrogant and start regretting things. You start making mistakes, losing duels, tricking people, and fighting against all authority—until finally you destroy the palace. The system collapses and there is a shortage of everything. After you start to abuse and sacrifice young girls, the people storm your estate. You are hunted, captured, divided, killed, and then tossed into a volcano by 'snake-demons'.

Pyramid (loc.)—Haiti.

"The Price of Power is insanity."
"To Survive is to depend on perversions of others."

15. "TO COMBINE" {conjoined twins}

Time—clock.
Space—city with large twin buildings.
Energy—explosion in laboratory.
Trouble—lobster-people.

Incident (track)—you are a genetic engineer (chemist/surgeon) of sorts, separating and combining "male" and "female" bodies to make 3-legged twin-forms. The basic body type is a pair of conjoined twins (born separately but combined to form a complete body). Normally, a "male" and "female" combine. The "males" only have one leg (and need crutches to walk); "female" bodies have two legs but require joining to a "male" in order to more fully exert themselves. After combining, the skin grows together, but may be separated again to allow a change in partners. Sex occurs between two sets of twins. You start by performing 7 brilliant operations that separate and combine twin-form bodies. Downscale, you make more outrageous combinations of people and animals (and forms that include more than two individuals). The 'lobster-people' protest this and try to make everyone 'singletons'. You change partners a few times, getting worse and worse ones; get blamed for riots and invasions of the 'lobster-people'; then hunted down as a 'singleton' and combined with a dead body. The incident ends with usual after-death sequence, &tc.

Pyramid (loc.) — southeastern *Atlantis.*

"The Price of Harmony is self-sacrifice."
"To Survive is to depend on the weakness of others."

16. "TO (BRING) ORDER" {gorilla people}

Note: might be *"To Align"*; might correspond to the *9th dynamic system "Ethics."*

Time—sun-shadows over village in snow.

Space—view of snow-covered mountains.

Energy—gorilla-person fighting with moose.

Mass—vast wall of snow about to fall.

Gods—totem pole (with living faces).

Crush—gorilla-person under an avalanche.

Injustice—individual sacrificed by group.

Incident (track)—you solve 7 major problems by getting people to change and align with each other (for group efforts). The village is in a flood area (come spring), so you get everyone to move and they are generally happy (though there are always occasional protestors you must overwhelm). Downscale, the changes are more arbitrary (or for personal gain) and you make mistakes. You overwhelm others by getting people to gang up on them. More people protest, and you label them as 'anti-social', but your justifications begin to break down. You regret things but carry on in order to make yourself right. You have your 'followers' kill your opponents, also causing many 'followers' to die. Eventually the people destroy the village and hunt for you in the forest, &tc.

Pyramid (loc.)—North Dakota.

"The Price of Order is obligation."
"To Survive is to depend on the xenophobia of others."

17. "TO REASON" {comic-clown}

Time—dial-clock on a tall skyscraper.
Space—the city at dusk.
God—crackling-cloud in power-plant.
Turmoil—incompetent police running
            around.
Sensation—woman in lingerie.

Companionship—woman in checkered
        apron.

Sex—exchanging energy sparks.

Incident (track)—the common body type is doll-bodies, with clothing built into the body. You are more intelligent than other people; you are something of a 'comic-character' so that they will like you anyways. You use brilliant logic to solve 7 difficult problems. Downscale, you use logic to persuade people to give you money, sex, &tc. Eventually, the people use your own logic against you; you become a tragic figure that traps and destroys yourself (according to your own "rules"). So you rebel and deny your logic; the people hunt you down. You are taken before the energy-god, a crackling-cloud in a power-plant, who divides you against yourself, &tc.

Pyramid (loc.)—South Africa.

"The Price of Logic is to entrap yourself."
"To Survive is to depend on the stupidity of others."

18. "TO ORIENT" {*wire man*}

Time—sun light/shadow moving across a
      structure in orbit.

Space—building a cage-like structure in
      space.

God—a statue of a man.

Body—made of thick wires that can bend.

Sex—bodies have a genital region
      (involving electrical plugs)

Incident (track)—you are a brilliant genius
who can see how to align wires in a structure for maximum efficiency. You are
building a complex cage-like structure in
space (orbiting a planet). This 'space
structure' tunes to the basic 'universal energy'. Increasing the structure (properly)
increases the flow and brings great
prosperity. Crowds cheer; priests honor,
&tc. The construct becomes too complex
and many mistakes are made (causing
bodies to be painfully shaken with 'bad
vibrations'). Eventually, you are taken to
the *god-statue* and divided, &tc.

Pyramid (loc.) — Antarctica.

"The Price of Orientation is to be stuck."

"To Survive is to depend on confidence from others."

19. "TO GUIDE" {*pilot*}

Time — a prairie at dusk.

Space — floating flatland continents.

Motion — "zeppelins" flying between floating continents.

God — statue in cathedral.

Impact — plane crash.

Guide — plane leading zeppelins through the clouds.

Incident (track) — you are a goggle-wearing pilot that flies a powerful airplane (only primitive in appearance because of the double-wings and open-cockpit). Early on there is some personal "levitation" ability, but this becomes problematic to control by the end. Transport "zeppelins" travel between continents and require planes to guide them. At the top, you guide 7 great convoys between flatworlds, earning admiration and esteem. Downscale, you become arrogant, demand too much money, cheat on your spouse, get drunk and lose some zeppelins in the sky, start crashing planes, and discover disorientation (dizziness). You take a young girl up in the plane, lose control, she dies, you fall. The people capture you and take you to the cathedral where the god-statue divides you. You try to fly afterward, but keep crashing, which is how you die. After being buried in a cemetery, 'winged-devils' throw you into a flat-earth volcano-hell where you are tortured by those you cheated/betrayed.

Pyramid (loc.)—Lemuria.

"The Price of Success is to be despised."

"To Survive is to depend on the good will of others."

20. "TO COMPUTE" {toy bodies}

Time—a toy clock.
Space—a logic-maze constructed of toys.

God—toy-master ("Santa Claus" type).

Sex—between toy-bodies.

Incident (track)—you are bright and your goal is to get through a logic maze (an elaborate labyrinth). At the top you solve 7 difficult problems; helping others; working deeply into the labyrinth. When you judge/evaluate an action wrong, your toy body gets smashed, requiring you to take a new one and start again. You start zapping troublesome toys with energy. Downscale, you start losing more bodies and get worried you'll never solve the maze. You trick others into trying things to avoid losing your own body. Getting worried someone else will surpass you, you start distributing false data, and change puzzles so that the answers don't work for those coming up behind you. Eventually the puzzles get rearranged to the point where you can no longer get as deeply into the labyrinth. You worry about running out of bodies and start to organize riots. Eventually, you are taken before the "toy-master" (Santa-like god) and divided. When you try to enter the maze again, each of your last toy-bodies are smashed; pieces are collected, buried, and held in place by "crosses" until 'devils' toss you into a volcano beneath the central part of the maze, &tc.

Pyramid (loc.)—Australia.

"The Price of Intelligence is self-destruction." *"To Survive is to depend on answers from others."*

21. "TO CONSTRUCT" {beaver-people}

Time—sun swings over the dam.
Space—dam village of beaver-people.
God—a river-spirit.
Sex—orgies in the mud.

Incident (track)—you are a beaver-person; squirrel-people are slave-laborers; skunk-people work as maid, &tc. You complete 7 large construction projects, such as managing the building of dams and fish-traps, and extending the village on planks out over the water. Downscale, the traps catch other people, who you then enslave and put to work. You start building traps for beaver-people too, so they rebel and take you to the 'river-lake-god' and are divided against yourself, &tc.

Pyramid (loc.) — Australia.

"The Price of Industriousness is entrapment."

"To Survive is to depend on the labor of others."

22. "TO ARRANGE" {blockhead}

Note: limited data blends with 22X.

22X. "TO ENGINEER" {lobster-people}

Time — mechanical clock (exposed gears).
Space — undersea domed city.
Energy — giant machines (pumps
        churning water).
Mass — underwater avalanche.

Incident (track) — you are a lobster-person and a brilliant engineering genius. At the top, you design 7 marvelous projects; but then you start altering designs for your own profit; things collapse; people die. Power-sources and other systems fail due to misengineering; riots start. When the people find out you are to blame, they chase and hunt you down, &tc.

Pyramid (loc.)—Africa.

"The Price of Calculation is to be detested."
"To Survive is to depend on the strength of others."

23. "TO BUILD" {snake people}

Time—sun in orbit.
Space—a "space city" (planet-sized
   construct).
Crash—'air-car' smashes into building.
Crush—'snake-person' under collapsing
   roadway.

Incident (track)—you undertake 7 projects to expand the fantastically complex and beautifully constructed 'space city'. You hurt slave-workers in the process (but justified it as 'for the higher good'). Then you start to have problems with construction errors, social unrest, and riots. Your building becomes too big and falls apart. Enraged citizens chase you through the sky, &tc.

Pyramid (loc.)—Bangkok.

"The Price of Having is enslavement."
"To Survive is to depend on the compulsions of others."

24. "TO STRUCTURE" {crystals}

Time—pulsing crystal.
Space—crystal city (rods and basic
   structures) suspended over a lake.
Energy—energy-flow blasts from crystal.
Shattered—crystal breaking apart.
Sex—sides of crystals in contact
   (rubbing); crackling-energy.
Body Type—levitating gems (that project
   energy, beams, &tc.) that survive
   on salts from the water and
   energy from sunlight.

Incident (track)—you undertake 7 projects extending the city higher into the sky and become highly admired. Downscale, you make mistakes and begin stealing sunlight from others. The poor must float up above the city to get their sunlight-energy, but live in deep shadows of the city, and gradually lack the energy to climb that high—so they begin breaking apart and dying. You help the rich build bigger levels, which makes it worse for the poor. Eventually societal systems fail, the city falls and mobs chase you, *&tc.*

Pyramid (loc.)—France.

"The Price of Alignment is to be held (located) in place."

"To Survive is to depend on the form of others."

25. "TO INVENT" {*dwarves or house-elves*}

Time—mechanical clock.

Space—large cluttered workshop.

Incident (track)—you are an eccentric inventor in a Bavarian or Dutch-style village. You invent 7 wondrous aesthetically pleasing things, including a fancy town clock. The inventions are so beautiful that they gain instant agreement. Downscale, greed, lust, and pride, cause you to maintain your position by inventing terrible (but aesthetic) devices to gain things— but also weapons of war and enslavement, originally for use against invading 'insect-people', but which get used to control the population. Eventually the mobs chase you down, &tc.

Pyramid (loc.)—Pennsylvania.

"The Price of Ingenuity is entrapment."

"To Survive is to depend on the aesthetic appreciation of others."

26. "TO ENHANCE" {ghost people}

Space—spirit world (city of ghosts) that intersects a late-19th Century styled material city.

God—man on a cross in a church.

Companionship—a male ghost.

Sensation—living male cat-person.

Body Types—humans and cat-people.

Incident (track)—you are a female spirit that enhances the view of things for living people. You cause 7 enhancements:

making guys seeing girls as more beautiful, disguising the drab appearance of the city, &tc. You visit living men in the night for sex and take a drop of blood as an offering, which makes you more 'real' (material) and stronger than the other ghost-people. You make everything seem better than it really is, and this gets people into trouble and leads them to mistakes. You become mischievous, haunt people, and even demand sacrifices. Priests attempt to 'exorcise' you; eventually capturing you and taking you before the god, who divides you against yourself, &tc.

Pyramid (loc.) — Buenos Aires.

"The Price of Improvement is condemnation."
"To Survive is to depend on the illusions of others."

27. "TO INSPIRE" {muses}

Time — a sundial.
Space — astral world intersecting a
             material world.
Trouble — knights with flaming swords

that can pierce the astral plane.

Disaster—earthquake.

You—female astral body.

Sensation—another female.

Incident (track)—At the top, you provide 7 wonderful inspirations and are praised. Downscale, you start running out of inspiring ideas, so you begin stealing them from other muses. Eventually, you start inspiring people toward crime, perversion, and cause nightmares. When you are thrown into the volcano at the end, escape becomes impossible because you have no new ideas (inspiration).

Pyramid (loc.)—Ethiopia.

"The Price of New Ideas is to be scorned."

"To Survive is to depend on the dullness of others."

28. "TO BEAUTIFY" {fairy godmother}

Time—sun swings.

Space—storybook land/kingdom.

Energy—beams from 'wand' makes things beautiful.

You—flying 'faerie queen'.

Incident (track)—you start by performing 7 amazing deeds, beautifying the landscape, the buildings and castle, and even making it so the poor girl can meet the prince; all very 'storybook' until you see that the people are messing up the environment and doing 'ugly' things. The girl gets her beautiful dress messed up having sex, so you give her a poisoned apple. Starving children eat the ornate 'gingerbread houses', so you throw them into a furnace. You gradually depopulate the kingdom and the people fear you—summoning 'witches' and 'devils' to capture and divide you, then keeping you bound under a magic circle until 'witches on broomsticks' fly you to the volcano.

Pyramid (loc.)—*Florida*.

"The Price of Beauty is sadness (suffering)."
"To Survive is to depend on the good taste of others."

29. "TO PURIFY" {fire people}

Time—sun swings.
Space—a fire-city of fire-people.
Mass—a central volcano.

Incident (track)—At the top, you find 7 horrible criminals using your ability to see the 'impurities' in their 'flame'; and they are captured and tossed into the central volcano. The people cheer. Eventually it becomes like the 'Inquisition' or 'Thought Policing', searching out anyone with 'impure thoughts'. You start making more mistakes, tossing in the wrong people and even 'good people' for personal gain. Finally, there is the inevitable ending with your capture, division, and volcano-torture experience, *&tc.*

Pyramid (loc.)—*Italy.*

"The Price of Purity is loss of self-determinism (individuality)."
"To Survive is to depend on the iniquity (impurity) of others."

30. "TO JUDGE" {minotaur}

Note: goal also may be *"To Arbitrate."*

Time—a sundial (in the plaza).

Space—a classical Grecian styled city.

Mass—building under construction
collapses on workers.

Body Type—'bull-people'

Incident (track)—you start by solving 7 great disputes, including one between the king and the slave-workers. You do this by talking to them and shifting their viewpoints, until they come to an agreement. Your ability to bring people into agreement through compromise is praised and rewarded. Downscale, this begins to bring harm to people, such as getting workers to compromise the safety of a building under construction, then it collapses on them. Eventually, everyone is losing too much through compromise, and they blame you, chase you down, &tc.

Pyramid (loc.)—*Buenos Aires.*

"The Price of Compromise is universal misery."
"To Survive is to depend on the obligations of others."

31. "TO DEFEND" {*aliens*}

Time—'flying-saucer' in orbit.
Space—a ship over the cities.
God—a silver robot.
Holy—"cross" on control panel.

Incident (track)—you succeed in 7 great battles, defending against evil invaders, revolutionaries, heretics, &tc. You realize that not all the 'rebels' are 'bad' and start regretting blasting them; but you continue in pride and duty. Downscale, you become arrogant and start blasting entire cities (of loyal people) once they are invaded by lizard-people. Social systems collapse and civilization crumbles. Rebel ships capture yours. They take you before the 'silver-robot' god, who divides you; and while you're allowed to return to your ship, the crew now despises you (considering you a traitor) and they throw you into the volcano, &tc.

Pyramid (loc.) — Tibet.

"*The Price of Ethics is betrayal.*"

"*To Survive is to depend on the integrity of others.*"

32. "TO STRENGTHEN" {*energy sphere*}

Note: may read as "*To Protect.*"

Space — a city of other body-types.

Energy — electricity.

You — a ball/sphere of colored energy.

Reward — being fed (in-flowing) electricity.

Sex — exchanging energy with other spheres.

Incident (track) — you police a city of other body-types. You start by handling 7 critical situations, protecting the innocent by 'zapping' their attackers. Downscale, you 'zap' the wrong people, mishandle situations, fight with other spheres, develop perversions (drinking in 'sex-energy flows' from bodies). You eventually become quite viscous. No longer being fed energy, you start stealing it, even draining it from bodies, and killing them, followed by typical end-sequence, *&tc*.

Pyramid (loc.)—Washington, D.C.

"The Price of Safety is inhibition."
"To Survive is to depend on the sins (misdeeds) of others."

33. "TO ENLIGHTEN" {rabbit preacher}

Note: might actually be *"To Preach."*
Time—sun-swings over countryside.
Space—country-town.
You—a 'rabbit-preacher'.
Holy—a book you carry.
Sacrifice—crucifixion (dying on a cross).
Body Types—'rabbit-people' (in dress coats); 'wolf-people' (in leather jackets).

Incident (track)—you preach 'sacrifice' to higher purposes. At the top, you work 7 miracles. Downscale, you sacrifice 'rabbit-people' to the 'wolf-people' (you preach to). You engage in secret cult-like orgies, and experience the usual sequence of decline and troubles; dying on a cross, &tc.

Pyramid (loc.) — *Alabama.*

"The Price of Preaching is sacrifice."
"To Survive is to depend on the faith of others."

34. "TO CONVERT" {*fish man*}

Time — sun-swings over lagoon.
Space — gulf coast (seashore/lagoon).
Gods — statues (main 'terminals' from other penalty-universes).
Worship — lesser-gods that demand sacrifice in return for small favors.
Holy — temples built on reefs.
You — reptilian fish-man (*Oannes, Dagon*).

Incident (track) — you have the ability to evoke 'heavenly pictures' in the sky (which are scenes from other penalty-universes), which allows you to promote a 'false religion', and convince others (even the 'lesser-gods') that you are an agent of a 'higher god'. You perform 7 wondrous acts, such as using the 'pictures' to stop wars and affect large events. But, unlike the 'lesser-gods', you can't really heal the sick, or control the weather, &tc. When the people start to catch on to this fact, you get into various troubles and experience the usual decline, &tc.

Pyramid (loc.)—southeastern *Atlantis.*

"The Price of Divine Revelation is to be fooled."

"To Survive is to depend on the gullibility of others."

35. "TO COMMUNE" {*female angel*}

Note: may read as *"To Connect."*

Time—sun on clouds.

Space—pearly/golden-gates and clouds.

Energy—golden-rays descending from 'God-on-high'.

Mass—golden altar in 'heavenly cathedral'.

Ecstasy—angels in the 'cathedral' writing in God's light (you receive religious and sexual ecstasy by direct connection/communion with God).

Sex—sharing 'ecstasy' with someone other than God (is forbidden).

Incident (track)—you have 7 divine religious and ecstatic experiences (usually in a group) in various locations (like the 'cathedral'), when "God's light" shines down. Downscale, you begin to do 'forbidden things', which causes you to 'hold-back'/'hold-out' (hide) from God when the bliss-light shines. You discover you can experience 'communion' and 'ecstasy' with those other than God through sex, which perverts many of the angels, causing many troubles. The 'sexual ecstasy' decays leaving only empty cravings. When you are found out, you argue with God and are cast out of the 'heavenly abode' onto the ground. You try to achieve 'sexual ecstasy' again through 'pain', but you become numb to this, die, *&tc.*

Pyramid (loc.)—*Hawaii.*

"The Price of Sensation is defilement."
"To Survive is to depend on others for fulfill-
ment."

36. "TO WORSHIP" {holy knights}

Time—sun-swings over forest and lake.
Space—castle overlooking lake and
meadow.
Energy—a 'holy knight' swinging
a sword.
Mass—the castle walls.
God—the 'God of the Cross'.
Worship—sacrificing to the 'God of the
Cross' (who absorbs the 'soul' of
people put on the 'Cross').

Incident (track)—you complete 7 holy
quests, like finding the holy grail. Downscale, you engage in 'crusades' against
rival religions, even smashing the
'statues' of their gods. When you start
feeling sympathy for your victims, and
guilt from your actions, you start betray-

ing your comrades, and there is the usual decline, &tc.

Pyramid (loc.)—China.

"The Price of Faith is blindness."
"To Survive is to depend on the blindness of others."

37. "TO PREDICT" {soothsayer}

Note: might actually be *To Predetermine*.
Time—sun shadow above a pasture.
Space—a flat-earth with mountains in the distance (resembling *Babylon/ Mesopotamia*).
God—the 'God in the Mountain'.
Body Types—material forms; and a 'symbol-body' that takes various forms, such as 'wise fool' (*tarot archetypes*), 'water-bearer' (*zodiac icons*), &tc.

Incident (track)—you can see the 'symbol-body' that is behind 'material-forms' and thereby know their destiny. You make prophecies based on these 'symbols', which further 'keys in' their significance and makes your predictions come to pass. You begin with making 7 great prophecies of doom, but you help the people to overcome the catastrophes. Downscale, you become more greedy and vengeful, predict false dooms, and speak out against kings. Eventually, the 'mountain god' divides you, &tc.

Pyramid (loc.)—Alberta, Canada.

"The Price of Prediction is to be foredoomed."
"To Survive is to depend on the superstitions of others."

38. "TO INFLUENCE" {cupid/cherub}

Space—in the 'clouds' above the cities.
God—god of the 'golden throne'.
Body Types—'cupid'-angels that live in the clouds, as do 'angels' and 'demons' (both of which object to the influence of the 'cupids'); body-types for people in the cities are from other penalty-universes.

Incident (track)—At the top, you visit 7 cities and inspire the people to experience 7 interesting emotions, and so the people (and other 'cupids') admire you. Down-scale, you inspire lower emotions—mise-motions like terror and hate—and eventually the people riot and tear civiliz-ation down. The angels capture you and drag you before the 'god of the golden-throne', who divides you against your-self. You die and are buried in a coffin-in-the-clouds for a time before the 'demons' haul you off to the volcano-hell, &tc.

Pyramid (loc.)—*Vermont.*

"The Price of Excitement is to stay hidden."
"To Survive is to depend on the discomfort of others."

39. "TO COLLECT" {elves/fairies}

Time—sun-swings over an elven 'forest-city'.
Space—field/clearing where fairies dance.
Energy—bolt from a 'ring of power'.
Mass—elves pushing a boulder.

Incident (track)—you are a great 'magical artificer' or 'spellsmith' that collects "beings." You capture 'spirits' and enchant them (surrounding them with your energy and crushing them) into material objects and weapons. When someone dies, you try to be nearby to 'collect' the 'spirit'. You begin by crafting 7 great devices, and are at first praised by the people. But they come to fear and despise you; and you grow vain and arrogant and start to hate everybody. The gods divide you against yourself; and when you die, you are 'collected' in an object and locked into a vault until being taken to the volcano-hell, &tc.

Pyramid (loc.) — Babylon/Baghdad (Iraq).

"The Price of Power is corruption."
"To Survive is to depend on the enslavement of others."

40. "TO EMBODY" {satyr/goat-god}

Note: initially researched as *"To Solidify."*
Time — sun-swings over forest glade.
Space — forest and brook.
Energy — geyser erupting from a lake.
Mass — 'dryads' melted into stone.

139

Evoke—playing 'pan-pipes' to summon the spirit out of a natural form, tree &tc.

Solidify—'dryad' outside of (exterior to) a tree, becoming solid.

Terror—bull-like 'demon' rising out of a lake (near a waterfall).

Trouble—'pinwheel' of energy around a silver cap.

God—'Guardian of the Forest' (tree-god).

Incident (track)—you start alone in a forest glade, using pan-pipes to evoke spirits from natural forms and solidifying them into a person—such as embodying the spirit of a tree as a 'dryad' or 'nymph', &tc. You evoke 7 groups of spirits and solidify them. They all praise and worship you and want their friends embodied as well. You populate the woods—occasionally evoking a 'monster' or 'demon' (or an 'energy pinwheel', which is dangerous to you). Downscale, you solidify things for your own gain, solidify beings against their will, demand payment from solidified beings, *&tc.* The forest starts dying (because you've pulled out all its spirits) and everyone blames you. They hunt you down, take you to the 'Guardian of the Forest', who divides you, *&tc.*

Pyramid (loc.)—Greece.

"The Price of Embodiment is suffering."
"To Survive is to depend on the harmony of others."

41. "TO DISCOVER" {centaurs}

Note: may also read as *"To Explore."*
Time—sun-swings over ship at sea.
Space—looking over railing of ship out at the shores of a bay.
Energy—a charging rhinoceros.
Mass—cliffs at shore; waves thrust a ship towards them.
Trouble—angels with flaming swords.
Body Types—you and your shipmates are horse-people (centaurs); body-types from other penalty-universes are also encountered.

Incident (track)—at the top, you are on an

explorer's ship sailing from bay to bay along the shores of a newly discovered continent. You intend to find treasure, learn native wisdom, and teach. You visit 7 bays, each inhabited by its own body-types (rabbit-people and robots; cat-people and bears; goat-people and elves; magicians and Sumerians; gnomes and giants; frog-people and insects; Olympian-type gods and dog-people). At first, the indigenous populations welcome you. Downscale, you try to dominate, exploit, and enslave them. You discover new ideas and try to teach them things, but they fail to listen—so you begin to trap them "for their own good" and force them into schools. They rebel; they pray for help; angels with fiery swords come to oppose you, destroy your ship, capture you, take you before god, &tc.

Pyramid (loc.)—South Africa.

"The Price of Discovery is blame."

"To Survive is to depend on the naivete of others."

42. "TO LOCATE" {leprechaun (wise fool)}

Time—a grandfather clock.

Space—a circular room plus the shadows of other rooms (interconnected at random; fourth spatial dimension).

Energy—a ray from the center passes into a room and hits someone.

Mass—someone pounding on the wall.

Boisterous—a drinking hall.

Incident (track)—you are a "locator" working for the king. There is a "sun" (surrounded by a balcony) in the center of the room that puts out higher-dimensional rays, which pass through walls of many interconnected rooms of a giant castle-keep. Unlike most others, you have the ability to sense the direction of the rays and know where things are in the rooms and halls that are constantly shifting in concentric rings around the central room. You start by going on 7 missions, successfully locating people and things, and are showered with praise and riches. Downscale, you start hiding things, concealing locations of treasure (for yourself), and get others lost. You start making too many mistakes and get yourself lost. The kingdom starts to fail; you are blamed; soldiers chase you. You finally end up in the volcano-hell under the floor, beneath the "sun" in the central room, &tc.

Pyramid (loc.)—Equador.

"The Price of Being Located is to be a target."
"To Survive is to depend on the mis-orientation of others."

43. "TO GATHER" {spacesuit body}

Note: limited data available for this IPU.
Body Type—faceless 'spacesuit' or
          'radiation suit' is the body.

Incident (track)—you use an 'implanting-device' on others, which uses the type of content described in "The Jewel of Knowledge" (AT Manual #3). You start by conquering 7 societies and are hailed a great leader. At first, you don't experience any regret in conquering 'meat-body' people; your deceit and betrayal concerns other 'invaders' like yourself. You start making mistakes, get overwhelmed by robots and revolutionaries, and start to lose your courage—followed by the usual decline, &tc.

Pyramid (loc.)—Atlantis.

"The Price of Wealth is to be controlled."
"To Survive is to depend on the 'conditionability' of others."

44. "TO OWN" {fox people}

Note: limited data blended with 44X.

44X. "TO PERMEATE" {spirit body}

Time—sun-shadows.

God—'centaur' (statue).

Incident (track)—as a spiritual-entity, you 'permeate' "meat-bodies" in order to 'implant'. You help the 'tiger-people' and 'fox-people' (&tc.), by 'blanketing' entire crowds and 'implanting' orders to stop riots, &tc. Downscale, you 'implant' for entertainment and personal gratification, but eventually inspire all the people to fight each other. After the centaur-statue god divides you against yourself, your future 'implant' attempts conflict with themselves and are ineffective.

Pyramid (loc.) — Saudi Arabia.

"The Price of Pervasion is dissolution."
"To Survive is to depend on the suggestibility of others."

45. "TO GROW" {genetic entity}

Note: this IPU-*incident* involves 'creation' and 'growth' before the usual decline, rather than starting at the 'top'.

Time — sea-organisms as day turns to
        night.
Space — a southsea volcanic island; bay,
        reefs, the sky above.
Energy — lightning-bolt striking, causing a
        forest-fire.
Mass — a rocky cliff above the beach.

Likingness—feeling tenderness toward a
mouse-like creature.

Reality—a volcano sheathed in clouds.

Communication—a monkey points a snake
out to another.

Understanding—two sloths are hanging
out together in the trees.

Fate—a glacier.

Help—amoeba reaching out to another
that is sinking.

Decay—fungus on a tree.

Creation—strange glow from a cave.

Warmth—a green sun in the sky.

Turbulence—waves.

Fall—bird dropping on a clam-shell.

Competition—another 'genetic-entity'
(blue colored).

Abandonment—shellfish on beach.

Doom—erupting volcano.

You—a 'genetic entity' (cloud-like
consciousness) attempting to
evolve your own 'genetic line' of
various organic forms, increasing
in complexity.

Incident (track)—you begin with simple lifeforms on a lifeless volcanic island, then gradually move on to more complex ones. You find yourself 'in competition' with a rival 'genetic-entity' on the other side of the island. You each begin evolving forms to eat or trample the other's newly made forms.

Pyramid (loc.)—Australia.

"The Price of Growth is death."
"To Survive is to depend on the sacrifices of others."

46. "TO LIVE" {dinosaur/saurian}

Note: might read as *"To Suffer."*

Note: too little data for this IPU.

47. "TO HEAL" {tree-man/forest-guardian}

Time—shifting slant of sunlight through the forest canopy.

Space—a path through the forest extending out to the distance.

Competition—another 'forest-guardian' (at the other side of the forest).

God—'mountain-god' (earth-god).

Trouble—'boar-person' (tusked pig-man).

Incident (track)—at the top, you visit 7 races (cat-people, bull-people, *&tc.*) and perform miraculous healing for each. They build altars to you; praise and worship you. You don't like them fighting with each other, so you try to control them. You push the 'injuries' back in on them when they disobey you, and they sicken and die. You find yourself in competition with another 'forest-guardian', and your people and theirs start fighting. Too many are hurt for you to heal them all, so your people turn against you—capturing you, and taking you to the 'mountain-god', who divides you, *&tc.*

Pyramid (loc.)—Uruguay.

"The Price of Healing is pain."
"To Survive is to depend on the weakness of others."

48. "TO ADAPT" {thread man}

Note: limited data available.

Time—a clock-tower (silver ball with
        streamers).

Space—city.

Energy—waves shake the city.

Mass—a great rock crushes things.

Trouble—'cyclops' (one-eyed giant), *&tc.*

Horror—'solidification' and 'burning'.

You—a 'thread-body'; a bundle of threads
        that can unravel and reweave into
        a different shape.

Incident (track)—at the start, you are highly adaptive and teach others to adapt to 7 significant threats—crab-people who chop with pincers; cyclops that burn you with their eye; bull-people that enforce rules.

Pyramid (loc.)—*Syria.*

49. "TO ESTABLISH" {3-eyed giants}

Note: limited data available.

Space—an electronic hyperspace (ultra-
        dimensional) grid that links 7
        'planes' or 'flatlands'.

Incident (track)—you establish 7 'flatlands'

with a race of beings ('children', 'fox-people', *&tc.*) on each, set up as a rigid caste system. Each race has a trade, task, or skill. You focus on establishing civilization by coordinating these diversities and expanding the 'space grid'. At the start, you have wonderful goals toward a vision of a glorious civilization. You 'implant' any dissenters "for the greater good." Downscale, people revolt; get too many 'implants'; you start committing too many harmful-acts, and finally give up on your involvement. When the civilization collapses, you are blamed, captured by a mob, *&tc.*

Pyramid (loc.) — Ireland.

"The Price of Order is invalidation."
"To Survive is to depend on the obedience of others."

50. "TO SHARE" {*dolphins*}

Time — sun-swings over ocean.
Space — dolphin in an air-glider (flying).
Energy — beam from sky boiling ocean.

Mass—dolphin in ocean levitating large
        amount of water.
God—giant statue of man holding trident.
Sex—orgies in the ocean.
Trouble—'insect-invaders' (type of 'alien').
Body Type—dolphin; no hands, but can
        levitate things by group postulate
        (shared 'alpha-thought').

Incident (track)—you share in 7 great co-operative efforts, including uprooting trees from the islands for wood, launching wooden spaceships, and even building a low-orbit platform (space-station). Agreements are forced by projecting 'thought bubbles' at one another. Eventually, you commit harmful-acts (as ordered by the group), including casting a friend off the space-platform—which causes you to rebel against the group and obsessively 'individuate'. You are taken before the 'sea-god' statue, who divides you, &tc.

Pyramid (loc.)—Azores.

"The Price of Sharing is enforced agreement."
"To Survive is to depend on the agreement of others."

51. "TO CONTROL" {frog king}

Note: potential errors in data.

Time—a water-clock (trays of water).

Space—a village of floating 'house-boats'.

Energy—a tidal wave.

Mass—cliffs overhanging the lake.

Sex—underwater breeding.

Trouble—'alien-invaders'.

Body Type—'frog-person'; mostly live in/ on the water; also have buildings on shore.

Incident (track)—you control the pond by leading and manipulating people, and even try to control other ponds. You perform 7 great acts of control, getting people to work together in such ways as to stop crime, construct dams, and fend off invaders. When the people won't obey your rules, you put "control helmets" on them which cause headaches when they disobey orders, break laws, or have thoughts against government. Eventually, you start to add 'invader-forces' in order to give you excuses for exercising more control. When your misdeeds are found out, the people rebel, chase you, &tc.

Pyramid (loc.)—Africa (Lake Nayassa).

"The Price of Civilization is oppression."
"To Survive is to depend on the meekness of others."

52. "TO UNITE" {dog soldiers}

Time—sun-swings over battlefield.
Space—a harbor with ships, planes, and troops amassed on the shore.
Energy—mushroom cloud (bomb blows up city).
Mass—giant steel doors of a fortress-like bunker.
God—statue of a giant bird on a pedestal.
Sex—with an enemy spy.
Trouble—'cat-people'.
You—'dog-person'; a soldier fighting in a

war for racial-purity (against the 'cat-people').

Incident (track)—as an officer, you engage in 7 glorious campaigns toward defeating the enemy, uniting countries, and purifying the race. At first you agree heavily with this, but then begin to question. The army installs 'control devices' in your teeth. You have sex with an enemy spy and begin to sympathize with the enemy (and start helping them). When you're found out, you flee to the enemy side, who implant more devices on you and send you back as a counter-spy. You're caught again, implanted further, *&tc.* After being divided against yourself, the 'hidden fragments' of yourself become active when you are asleep—continuing to report, *&tc.* Eventually, you disable the 'shields' and blow everyone up. Betrayed comrades from both sides pull you out of the grave, toss you in the volcano, *&tc.*

Pyramid (loc.)—*Australia.*

"The Price of Loyalty is dishonor."
"To Survive is to depend on the honor of others."

53. "TO ORGANIZE" {*file clerk ('human')*}

Time—beeping computer signal (flashing red light on console).

Space—looking down at a cafeteria (incident is entirely indoors).

Energy—basket of forms thrown at a clerk's head.

Mass—endless piles of forms stacked to the ceiling.

God—an administrative computer.

Sex—an office privilege (a source of upset); done to you by seniors, by you to juniors.

Trouble—'bull-people'.

You—hermaphroditic file-clerk with the goal of putting order into everything; populations and planets are being taken over (which you handle with 'paperwork').

Incident (track)—at the start, you organize

7 departments, creating new forms and procedures to handle the ever growing piles of data. This operates on pure bureaucracy, including forms about forms. The penalty for mistakes is paying more taxes—which requires a horrific chain of forms in itself. Some people begin to starve and die because of the chain of forms required. The 'bull-people' are intolerable to this and start wrecking things. You feel guilty but continue. Angry mobs storm through the building setting fires to paperwork. When you are caught, you are taken before the 'computer-god' and divided. You die from falling down an elevator shaft, which leads to a large basement cavern and a volcano-hell, &tc.

Pyramid (loc.)—Portugal.

"The Price of Order is frustration."
"To Survive is to depend on the uniformity of others."

54. "TO COOPERATE" {robots}

Time—sunlight moving across a space-station.

Space—two large wheel-style space-stations; a planet they orbit; 7 large platforms, ships, robots moving about.

Energy—ship smashing into station; debris flying around.

Mass—large bundle of 'girders' drifting into a 'bulkhead' and crumpling it in a gravityless 'loading dock'.

God—a computer.

Creator—an octopus-type being in a tank of gas.

Dissolve—robots tossing others into a vat of boiling acid.

Conflict—warring space-stations in orbit; 'blue robots' versus 'red robots'.

Incident (track)—you do 7 significant projects, cooperating with other 'robots' to build things, expand the space-station, and fight enemy 'robots'. You act as a sort of 'team-leader' that gets others to work together, but they get in each others way —and you harm them for the sake of accomplishing the project, without any other regard. When the others get upset, you have them 'programmed' ('implanted'), again in the name of the project or for the sake of the group. Later you become disillusioned to 'purposes', and start to work only for yourself (own gain). You want to overthrow society, but can't because the other 'robots' will destroy everyone. When your evil intentions (thoughts) are found out, they drag you before the 'computer-god', &tc.

Pyramid (loc.)—Detroit/Michigan.

"The Price of Agreement is obedience."
"To Survive is to depend on the obedience of others."

55. "TO PARTICIPATE" {*merfolk*}

Note: potential errors in data.
Time—moon-swings above a mermaid on a rock at sea.

Space—undersea castle; luminescent fish swimming around.

Energy—ship crashing against the rocks.

Mass—heavy chest sinking in the water (mermaids struggling to pull it up, but fail).

God—giant statue of man with trident (half-exposed above the water).

Sex—causes fin-tail to split and develop legs.

Degradation—to have legs; confined to land.

Sympathy—displaying to others "what they've done to me."

Trouble—'centaurs' (horse-men on ship).

You—'mermaid'; your voice has 'magical powers' (amplified when singing with others).

Incident (track)—you participate in 7 significant group activities—such as singing, which compels 'human' sailors to crash on the rocks (and their stuff can be looted). Sometimes a ship has 'centaurs' (instead of 'humans') that can resist your voice (and they have magic of their own) and occasionally hunt you. You eventually have sex with a human, develop legs, and are cast out of 'merfolk' society. You then participate with other 'exiled mermaids' from on a shore, still sinking ships. The 'centaurs' finally catch you and take you before the 'god-statue', &tc.

Pyramid (loc.)—northeast *Lemuria*.

"The Price of Approval is self-degradation."
"To Survive is to depend on sympathy from others."

56. "TO EXPAND" {railroad engineer}

Note: limited data available.

Time—railroad clock-tower over station.

Space—train shed.

Energy—locomotive in motion.

Mass—coaling-tower dumping tons of coal.

God—a patriotic old-man wearing a top-hat.

Trouble—female 'doll-bodies' that shoot
  beams from eyes.

You—'mouse-person'; engineer of a vast
  rail-system (in competition).

Incident (track)—at the top you organize 7
great projects. Your railroads use red engines (and your competition uses green
engines) and you strategically work to
become the larger, more successful, rail-
system. Downscale, your rail-system becomes too complex and you start committing harmful-acts. Everyone struggles to
manage, the mice are worked to death,
&tc.

Pyramid (loc.)—*Philadelphia/Pennsylvania.*

"*The Price of Expansion is confusion.*"

"*To Survive is to depend on the toil of others.*"

57. "TO JOIN" {*cat people*}

Time—sun-swings over post-modern
  'cube' city.

Space—'cat-person' floating over an
  ocean.

162

Energy—a levitating 'cat-person'.

Mass—an iron chest that falls and crashes on the floor.

God—a voluptuous 'earth-mother' statue; many arms, holding many children, fed by many breasts.

Joining—sex.

Sex—'cat-people' are exhilarated about sex; have endless kids, but throw them out or kill them, until 'robots' enforce their care and feeding (which is painful on the body).

Trouble—'robots'.

Incident (track)—At the top you have 7 wonderful 'joinings'; but when you have litters of children, you kill them or throw them out to starve. 'Robots' come and enforce you having to 'nurse' your children. You continue downscale, violating laws, killing children, betraying lovers, engaging in sexual abuses, fighting 'robots', &tc. Eventually, the 'robots' take you to the 'mother-goddess' statue, which divides you against yourself with a beam. This fragmentation causes you to age and become ugly so that no males will 'join' with you anymore. You jump off a building and find you can no longer 'levitate' and smash in to the ground. The 'robots' scrape up the pieces of the body and lock them in a drawer that is electronically sealed. They take you out to sea and throw you into the volcano-hell, &tc.

Pyramid (loc.) — Babylon/Baghdad.

"The Price of Love is betrayal."

"To Survive is to depend on the lusts of others."

58. "TO REPRODUCE" {insect invader}

Time — wristwatch worn by 'insect-body'.

Space — 'insect-invaders' swooping down
      on a valley.

Energy — 'gorilla-people' with laser-
      cannon blast a cliff (with
      'insect-invaders' at the top of it).

Mass — spaceship sinking in the mud.

God—a giant stone-spider.

Trouble—'gorilla-people'.

Incident (track)—at the start, you participate as part of an 'invader-force' against 7 different planets. You come down from orbit riding prone on a small torpedo-shaped object with handlebars. You have wings that can support you, but cause you to tire easily. The goal is to populate the whole of the universe with your species, injecting eggs into the natives (different body-types). Some of the more technologically advanced species object to being 'egg-victims'. They give you trouble (and eventually catch you). You come to realize that your whole life is a harmful act. The 'gorilla-people' burn off your wings and drop you in a volcano, *&tc.*

Pyramid (loc.)—*Buenos Aires.*

"The Price of Expansion is starvation (detestation)."

"To Survive is to depend on the bodies of others."

59. "TO SATISFY" {*cavemen*}

Time—sun-shadows creeping across
      valley.

Space—looking down at valley from
      rocks.

Energy—'caveman' bashing head of
      mammoth with a club.

Mass—a gigantic rock.

God—'mammoth-god' statue.

Crush—arm sticking out from under the
      body of a mammoth.

Sensation (Satisfaction)—sex.

Trouble—'elves'.

You—'caveman'; you start as master of
      the land; hunt mammoths,
      kill bears, *&tc.*

Incident (track)—at the top, you successfully mate with 7 women, but each wants
to keep you for themselves, and things
begin deteriorating. One woman drives
off the others. You decide you want to
mate with one from another tribe, but she
isn't interested in you—so you drag them

off to your cave and break their legs so they can't get away. There are also 'elves' nearby. You chase them through caves and tunnels, catch 'elf-girls'; rape, &tc. But the 'elves' have magic and strike you with energy-bolts. They catch you and take you before the 'mammoth-god', who divides you against yourself. Now, no women want you, you can't catch animals, and 'elf-girls' throw rocks at you. Eventually, they roll a boulder onto you, and you die, &tc.

Pyramid (loc.)—France.

"The Price of Pleasure is sin."

"To Survive is to depend on pleasure from others."

60. "TO CARE (FOR)" {bird girl}

Time—'bird-girl' on porch of tree-house
       looking at sunset.

Space—'bird-girl' perched on large tree-
       branch overlooking giant trees of
       a forested valley.

Energy — 'bird-girl' flying fast up to the top of a cliff.

Mass — gigantic rock outcropping over valley (starting to crack off).

God — 'snake-god'; creature in a large bottle.

Trouble — 'snake-people'.

You — 'bird-girl'; you protect the forest; strangle trappers, &tc.

Incident (track) — you have 7 families of children (your own and other types of creatures, including dinosaurs/'saurians'), which you take great pleasure in successfully caring for. Although they greatly love you, they all insist on fighting and hurting one another. You try to make everyone stop fighting, but they resent this. You interfere with the 'snake-people' that enslave others, cut down trees to build vast structures and other things you loathe. They hunt you. Downscale, you try to stop everyone from doing anything — and begin killing anything that moves (all "for good reasons"). You've become the ultimate oppressor, so that no one is able to live anymore. Toward the end, the 'snake-people' promise to stop fighting, but they betray you. Eventually all of the children hand you over to the 'snake-people', who take you before the 'snake-god,' &tc.

Pyramid (loc.) — Africa.

"The Price of Caring is grief."
"To Survive is to depend on the suffering of others."

61. "TO EXPERIENCE" {*bear*}

Note: may read as *"To Feel"* or *"To Live."*
Time — sun-swings over snow-covered forest.
Space — a snowy mountain slope.
Difficult — 'bear' trying to catch fish.
God — 'forest-god' ('tree-man') statue.
Trouble — 'fox-people' (hunters).
You — 'bear'; animal (not 'bear-person').

Incident (track) — at the top, you are the master of all you survey, experiencing 7 wonderful feelings — climbing trees, scaring other animals, catching fish, having sex, eating honey, &tc. When it gets cold, you hibernate. Sometimes you get stung by bees. You start to mess things up in the forest, but you think it's a lot of fun. Hunters ('fox-people' with rifles) chase you. When you burn down part of the forest, you anger the 'forest-god'. He takes a spirit-form and catches you, takes you to his altar, and divides you, &tc. Now everything is terrible; you age; hunters kill you, skin you, and bury the bones. You can't get out of the grave until the 'devils' come; volcano-hell, &tc.

Pyramid (loc.)—Wisconsin.

"The Price of Sensation is pain."
"To Survive is to depend on others for sensation."

62. "TO REPLENISH" {a Sumerian}

Time—sunset in the desert.
Space—sitting on rocks looking at sand.
Energy—hurling a spear.
Mass—mountains in the distance.

170

Trouble—'spider-people'.

You—'Mesopotamian'; desert-dweller.

Incident (track)—you are sly and stealthy (like a 'thief' or 'rogue') and take what you want with great exhilaration. You complete 7 great successful thefts to replenish the tribe's coffers—such as finding and stealing a great treasure in the mountains. Downscale, you develop certain considerations about taking things from others, or using their energy, and you get tired. You happen upon a 'robot' base in the mountains and steal from them and get in trouble. Eventually, the 'spider-people' (the 'invaders' that own the 'robots') catch you and take you before their 'computer-god', who divides you against yourself. Now, you age rapidly and stagger about the mountains as an old-man, die, *&tc.*

Pyramid (loc.)—China.

"The Price of Motion is tiredness." Might read as *"The Price of Strength is exhaustion."*

"To Survive is to depend on others for sensation."

63. "TO EAT" {*tiger*}

Time—sun-swings over jungle.

Space—'tiger' looking over the jungle.

Energy—'tiger' leaping between rocks.

Mass—'tiger' watching 'natives' struggle
to lift a water-buffalo.

Motion—a large boulder rolls down a hill.

Food—a gray 'monkey' sitting in tall
grass.

Eating—a 'tiger' biting a gray 'monkey'.

God—giant monkey-god statue.

Trouble—'natives' (dark-skinned human).

Dizzy—stumbling around a water-hole.

Roar—brown 'tiger' roars at an 'elephant'.

You—'tiger'; animal (not 'tiger-person').

Incident (track)—you're a 'tiger' in the jungle. You eat 7 monkeys and gain great strength and aliveness. Downscale, you have trouble with 'natives', 'elephants', 'rhinos', &tc. The 'natives' capture and cage you, then take you to their 'monkey-god', who divides you against yourself. Now you age, struggle, and starve. When you die, the 'natives' dance on your grave so you can't get out. Then 'demon-birds' come and carry you to the volcano, &tc.

Pyramid (loc.)—India.

"The Price of Energy is guilt."
"To Survive is to depend on the energy of others."

64. "TO ENDURE" {pyramid}

Note: may read as *"To Persist."*

Time—sun-swings over 'pyramid with eye'.

Space—desert; a city in the distance.

Energy—beam coming out of 'pyramid'.

Mass—bricks that make up the 'pyramid'.

Danger—spaceship approaching 'pyramid'.

Trouble—an 'old-man' carrying a staff.

Hurt—sandstorm wearing away 'pyramid'.

Pain—beam from ship knocks off bricks.

Control—'eye of pyramid' shoots a beam
into eye of person.

Influence—a beam from 'pyramid'
blankets the city.

You—a stationary 'pyramid' (god-like, but
immobile); one 'eye' on each side
(each with a different function);
your influence permeates the
nearby city and the people
worship you.

Incident (track)—at the start, you do 7
wondrous things to help the city, but you
come to hypnotize rulers, play games
with people, and use them like toys.
There are other pyramids that you can in-
tertwine energies with for sensation, but
all feeling is quite numb—except the pain
of deterioration which is worrisome. As
parts of the 'pyramid' crumble, you hypnotize people to fix and rebuild it. When
you find yourself in competition with another 'pyramid', the two of you start a
'civil war', hypnotizing people to fight

against each other. Once you are successful getting the people to destroy the other 'pyramid', you realize that it is possible to die. A staff-carrying 'prophet' (that is immune to your hypnosis) calls down the 'sky gods' (giant humanoid spirits), which divide you against yourself. Now the people cease to worship you. You decay and are buried by the sand until you are eventually thrown into a volcano-hell, &tc.

Pyramid (loc.)—New York.

"The Price of Endurance is to be weighed down."

"To Survive is to depend on care from others."

Your next Advanced Training manual is:
"Entities & Fragments"

BASIC SYSTEMOLOGY GLOSSARY

actualization : to make actual, not just potential; to bring into full solid Reality; to realize fully in *Awareness* as a "thing."

agreement (reality) : unanimity of opinion of what is "thought" to be known; an accepted arrangement of how things are; things we consider as "real" or as an "is" of "reality"; a consensus of what is real as made by standard-issue (common) participants; what an individual contributes to or accepts as "real"; in *Systemology*, a synonym for "*reality.*"

alpha : the first, primary, basic, superior or beginning of some form; in *Systemology*, referring to the state of existence operating on spiritual archetypes and postulates, will and intention "exterior" to the low-level condensation and solidarity of energy and matter as the 'physical universe' (*beta*).

alpha-spirit : a "spiritual" *Life*-form; the "true" *Self* or I-AM; the *individual*; the spiritual (*alpha*) *Self* that is animating the (*beta*) physical body or "*genetic vehicle*" using a continuous *Lifeline* of spiritual ("*ZU*") energy; an individual spiritual (*alpha*) entity possessing no physical mass or measurable waveform (motion) in the Physical Universe as itself, so it animates the (*beta*) physical body or "*genetic vehicle*" as a catalyst to experience *Self*-determined causality in effect within the *Physical Universe*; a singular unit or point of *Spiritual Awareness* that is *Aware* that it is *Aware*.

alpha thought : the highest spiritual *Self-determination* over creation and existence exercised by an Alpha-Spirit; the Alpha range of pure *Creative Ability* based on direct postulates and considerations of *Beingness*; spiritual qualities comparable to "thought" but originating in Alpha-existence, independently superior to a Mind-System.

ascension : actualized *Awareness* elevated to the point of true "spiritual existence" exterior to *beta existence*. An "Ascended Master" is one who has returned to an incarnation on Earth as an inherently *Enlightened One*, demonstrable in their words and actions; they have the ability to *Self-direct* the "Mind" and "Body" as *Self* (as a "Spirit"); and to maintain consciousness as a personal identity continuum with the same *Self-directed* control and communication of Will-Intention that is exercised, actualized and developed deliberately during one's present incarnation.

associative knowledge : significance or meaning of a facet or aspect assigned to (or considered to have) a direct relationship with another facet; to connect or relate ideas or facets of existence with one another; in traditional systems logic, an equivalency of significance or meaning between facets or sets that are grouped together, such as in *(a + b) + c = a + (b + c)*; in Systemology, erroneous associative knowledge is assignment of the same value to all facets or parts considered as related (even when they are not actually so), such as in *a = a, b = a, c = a* and so forth without distinction.

attention : active use of *Awareness* toward a specific aspect or thing; the act of "attending" with the presence of *Self*; a direction of focus or concentration of *Awareness* along a particular channel or conduit or toward a particular terminal node or communication termination point; the Self-directed concentration of personal energy as a combination of observation, thought-waves and consideration; focused application of *Self-Directed Awareness*.

awareness : the highest sense of-and-as *Self* in knowing and being as I-AM (the *Alpha-Spirit*); the extent of beingness directed as a viewpoint (POV) experienced by *Self* as *Knowingness*.

beta (awareness) : all consciousness activity ("*Awareness*") in the "Physical Universe" (KI, in *Zuism*) or else in *beta-existence*; *Awareness* within the range of the *genetic-body*, including material thoughts, emotional responses and physical motors; personal *Awareness* of physical energy and physical matter moving through physical space and experienced as "time"; the *Awareness* held by *Self* that is restricted to an organic *Lifeform* or "*genetic vehicle*" in which it experiences causality in *beta-existence*.

beta (existence) : all manifestation in the "Physical Universe" (KI, in *Zuism*); the conditions of *Awareness* for the *Alpha-spirit* (*Self*) as a physical organic *Lifeform* or "*genetic vehicle*" in which it experiences causality in the *Physical Universe*.

charge : to fill or furnish with a quality; to supply with energy; to lay a command upon; in *Systemology*—to imbue with intention; to overspread with emotion; personal energy stores and significances entwined as fragmentation in mental images, reactive-response encoding and intellectual (and/or) programmed beliefs.

channel : a specific stream, course, current, direction or route; to form or cut a groove or ridge or otherwise guide along a specific course; a direct path; an artificial aqueduct created to connect two water bodies or water or make travel possible.

circuit : a circular path or loop; a closed-path within a system that allows a flow; a pattern or action or wave movement that follows a specific route or potential path only; in *Systemology*, "*communication processing*" pertaining to a specific *flow* of energy or information along a channel; "*feedback loop.*"

communication : successful transmission of information, data, energy (&tc.) along a message line, with a reception of feedback; an energetic flow of intention to cause an effect (or duplication) at a distance; the personal energy moved or acted upon by will or else 'selective directed attention'; the 'messenger action' used to transmit and receive energy across a medium; also relay of energy, a message or signal—or even locating a personal POV (viewpoint) for the Self—along the *ZU-line*.

condense (condensation) : the transition of vapor to liquid; denoting a change in state to a more substantial or solid condition; leading to a more compact or solid form.

confront : to come around in front of; to be in the presence of; to stand in front of, or in the face of; to meet "face-to-face" or "face-up-to"; additionally, in *Systemology*, to fully tolerate or acceptably withstand an encounter with a particular manifestation without an automatic reactive response.

consideration : careful analytical reflection of all aspects; deliberation; determining the significance of a "thing" in relation to similarity or dissimilarity to other "things"; evaluation of facts and importance of certain facts; thorough examination of all aspects related to, or important for, making a decision; the analysis of consequences and estimation of significance when making decisions; also in *Systemology*, the *postulate* or *Alpha-Thought* that defines the state of *beingness* for what something "*is*."

defragmentation : the *reparation* of wholeness; collecting all dispersed parts to reform an original whole; a process of removing "*fragmentation*" in data or knowledge to provide a clear understanding; applying techniques and processes that promote a *holistic* interconnected *alpha* state, favoring observational *Awareness* of continuity in all spiritual and physical systems; in *Systemology*, a "*Seeker*" achieving actualized "*Self-Honest Awareness*" is said to be in a basic state of *beta-defragmentation*, whereas *Alpha-defragmentation* is the rehabilitation of the *creative ability*, managing the *Spiritual Timeline* and the POV of *Self* as Alpha-Spirit (I-AM).

existence : the *state* or fact of *apparent manifestation*; the resulting combination of the Principles of Manifestation: consciousness, motion and substance; continued *survival*; that which independently exists.

exterior : outside of; on the outside; in *Systemology*, we mean specifically the POV of *Self* that is *'outside of'* the *Human Condition,* free of the physical and mental trappings of the Physical Universe; a metahuman range of consideration; see also *'Zu-Vision'*.

external : a force coming from outside; information received from outside sources; in *Systemology*, the objective *'Physical Universe'* existence, or *beta-existence*, that the Physical Body or *genetic vehicle* is essentially *anchored* to for its considerations of locational space-time as a dimension or POV.

fragmentation : breaking into parts and scattering the pieces; the *fractioning* of wholeness or the *fracture* of a holistic interconnected *alpha* state, favoring observational *Awareness* of perceived connectivity between parts; *discontinuity*; separation of a totality into parts; in *Systemology*, a person outside of *Self-Honesty* is said to be operating from a *fragmented* state.

flow : movement across (or through) a channel (or conduit); a direction of active energetic motion, typically distinguished as either an *in-flow*, *out-flow* or *cross-flow*.

genetic-vehicle : a physical *Life*-form; the physical (*beta*) body that is animated/controlled by the (*Alpha*) *Spirit* using a continuous *Spiritual Lifeline* (ZU); a physical (*beta*) organic receptacle and catalyst for the (*Alpha*) *Self* to operate "causes" and experience "effects" within the *Physical Universe*.

harmful-act : a counter-survival mode of behavior or action (esp. that causes harm to one of more *Spheres of Existence*)—or—an overtly aggressive (hostile and/or destructive) action against an individual or any other *Sphere of Existence*; in *Utilitarian Systemology*—a shortsighted (serves fewest/lowest *Spheres of Existence*) intentional overtly harmful action to resolve a perceived problem; a revision of the rule for standard *Utilitarianism* for Systemology to distinguish actions which provide the least benefit to the least number of *Spheres of Existence*, or else the greatest harm to the greatest number of *Spheres of Existence*; in *moral philosophy*—an action which can be experienced by few and/or which one would not be willing to experience for themselves (*theft, slander, rape, &tc*); an iniquity or iniquitous act.

hold-back : withheld communications (esp. actions) such as "*Hold-Outs*"; intentional (or automatic) withdrawal (as opposed to reach); Self-restraint (which may eventually be enforced or automated); not reaching, acting or expressing, when one should be; an ability that is now restrained (on automatic) due to inability to withhold it on Self-determinism alone.

hold-outs : in photography, the numerous snap-shots/pictures withheld from the final display or professional presentation of the event; withheld communications; in Utilitarian Systemology—energetic withdrawal and communication breaks with a "*terminal*" and its *Sphere of Existence* as a result of a "*Harmful-Act*"; unspoken or undiscovered (hidden, covert) actions that an individual withholds communications of, fearing punishment or endangerment of *Self-preservation* (*First Sphere*); the act of hiding (or keeping hidden) the truth of a "*Harmful-Act*"; a refusal to communicate with a *Pilot*; also "*Hold-Back.*"

holistic : the examination of interconnected systems as encompassing something greater than the *sum* of their "parts."

Human Condition : a standard default state of Human experience that is generally accepted to be the extent of its potential identity (*beingness*) —currently treated as *Homo Sapiens Sapiens,* but which is scheduled for replacement by *Homo Novus* (the "New Human").

imagination : ability to create *mental imagery* in one's Personal Universe at will and change or alter it as desired; the ability to create, change and dissolve mental images on command or as an act of will; to create a mental image or have associated imagery displayed (or "conjured") in the mind that may or may not be treated as real (or memory recall) and may or may not accurately duplicate objective reality; to employ *creative abilities* of the Spirit that are independent of reality agreements with beta-existence.

imprint : to strongly impress, stamp, mark (or outline) onto a softer 'impressible' substance; to mark with pressure onto a surface; in *Systemology*, used to indicate permanent Reality impressions marked by frequencies, energies or interactions experienced during periods of emotional distress, pain, unconsciousness, loss, enforcement, or something antagonistic to physical (personal) survival, all of which are are stored with other reactive response-mechanisms at lower-levels of *Awareness* as opposed to the active memory database and proactive processing center of the Mind; an experiential "memory-set" that may later resurface—be triggered or stimulated artificially—as Reality, of which similar responses will be engaged automatically; holographic-like imagery "stamped" onto consciousness as composed of energetic *facets* tied to the "snap-shot" of an experience.

imprinting incident : the first or original event

instance communicated and *emotionally encoded* onto an individual's "*Spiritual Timeline*" (recorded memory from all lifetimes), which formed a permanent impression that is later used to mechanistically treat future contact on that channel; the first or original occurrence of some particular *facet* or mental image related to a certain type of *encoded response*, such as pain and discomfort, losses and victimization, and even the acts that we have taken against others along the *Spiritual Timeline* of our existence that caused them to also be *Imprinted*.

intention : directed application of Will; to intend (have "in Mind") or signify (give "significance" to) for or toward a particular purpose; in *Systemology* (from the *Standard Model*)—the spiritual activity at WILL (5.0) directed by an *Alpha Spirit* (7.0); the application of WILL as "Cause" from a higher order of Alpha Thought and consideration (6.0).

interior : inside of; on the inside; in *Systemology*, we mean specifically the POV of *Self* that is fixed to the *'internal' Human Condition,* including the *Reactive Control Center* (RCC) and Mind-System or *Master Control Center* (MCC); within *beta-existence*.

internal : a force coming from inside; information received from inside sources; in *Systemology*, the objective experience of *beta-existence* associated with the Physical Body or *genetic vehicle* and its POV regarding sensation and perception; from inside the body; in the body.

invalidate : decrease the level or degree or *agreement* as Reality.

mental image : a subjectively experienced "picture" created and imagined into being by the Alpha-Spirit (or at lower levels, one of its automated mechanisms) that includes all perceptible *facets* of totally immersive scene, which may be forms originated by an individual, or a "facsimile-copy" ("snap-shot") of something seen or encountered; a duplication of wave-forms in one's Personal Universe as a "picture" that mirror an "external" Universe experience, such as an *Imprint*.

perception : internalized processing of data received by the *senses*; to become *Aware of* via the senses.

pilot : a professional steersman responsible for healthy functional operation of a ship toward a specific destination; in *Systemology*, an intensive trained individual qualified to specially apply *Systemology Processing* to assist other *Seekers* on the *Pathway*.

point-of-view (POV) : a point to view from; an opinion or attitude as expressed from a specific identity-phase; a specific standpoint or vantage-point; a definitive manner of consideration specific to an individual phase or identity; a place or position affording a specific view or vantage; circumstances and programming of an individual that is conducive to a particular response, consideration or belief-set (paradigm); a position (consideration) or place (location) that provides a specific view or perspective (subjective) on experience (of the objective).

postulate : to put forward as truth; to suggest or assume an existence *to be*; to state or affirm the existence of particular conditions; to provide a basis of reasoning and belief; a basic theory accepted as fact; in *Systemology*, Alpha-Thought —the top-most decisions or considerations made by the Alpha-Spirit regarding the "*isness*" (what things "are") about energy-matter and space-time.

presence : a quality of some thing (*energy/matter*) being "present" in space-time; personal orientation of *Self* as an *Awareness* (*POV*) located in present space-time (environment) and communicating with extant energy-matter.

processing command line (PCL) : a directed input; a specific command using highly selective language for *Systemology Processing*; a predetermined directive statement (cause) intended to focus concentrated attention (effect).

processing, systematic : the inner-workings or "through-put" result of systems; in *Systemology*, a method of applied spiritual technology used toward personal Self-Actualization; methods of selective directed attention, communicated language and associative imagery that increases personal control of the human condition.

realization : the clear perception of an understanding; a consideration or understanding on what is "actual"; to make "real" or give "reality" to so as to grant a property of "beingness" or "being as it is"; the state or instance of coming to an *Awareness*; in *Systemology*, "gnosis" or true knowledge achieved during *systematic processing*; achievement of a new (or higher) cognition, true knowledge or perception of Self; a consideration of reality or assignment of meaning.

responsibility : the *ability* to *respond*; the extent of mobilizing *power* and *understanding* an individual maintains as *Awareness* to enact *change*; the proactive ability to *Self-direct* and make decisions independent of an outside authority.

Seeker : an individual on the *Pathway to Self-Honesty*; a practitioner of *Mardukite Systemology* or *Systemology Processing*, that is working toward *Spiritual Ascension*.

Self-actualization : bringing the full potential of the Human spirit into Reality; expressing full capabilities and creativeness of the *Alpha-Spirit*.

Self-determinism : the freedom to act, clear of external control or influence; the personal control of Will to direct intention.

Self-honesty : the basic or original *alpha* state of *being* and *knowing*; clear and present total *Awareness* of-and-as *Self*, in its most basic and true proactive expression of itself as *Spirit* or *I-AM*—free of artificial attachments, perceptive filters and other emotionally-reactive or mentally-conditioned programming imposed on the human condition by the systematized physical world; the ability to experience existence without judgment.

spiritual timeline : a continuous stream of moment-to-moment *Mental Images* (or a record of experiences) that defines the "past" of a spiritual being (or *Alpha-Spirit*) and which includes impressions (*imprints, &tc.*) from all life-incarnations and significant spiritual events the being has encountered; in Systemology, also "*backtrack.*"

Spheres of Existence : a series of *eight* concentric circles, rings or spheres (each larger than the former) that is overlaid onto the Standard Model of Beta-Existence to demonstrate the dynamic systems of existence extending out from the POV of Self (often as a "body") at the *First Sphere*; these are given in the basic eightfold systems as: *Self, Home/Family, Groups, Humanity, Life on Earth, Physical Universe, Spiritual Universe* and *Infinity-Divinity.*

Systemology : a modern tradition of applied religious philosophy and spiritual technology based on *Arcane Tablets* (in combination with *"general systemology"* and *"games theory"*) developed in the New Age underground by Joshua Free in 2011 as an advanced futurist extension of the *Mardukite Research Org.*

terminal (node) : a point, end, or mass, on a line; a connection point for closing an electric circuit, such as a post on a battery terminating at each end of its own systematic function; a point of connectivity with other points; in systems, a contact point of interaction; a point of interaction with other points.

turbulence : a quality or state of distortion or disturbance that creates irregularity of a flow or pattern; the quality or state of aberration on a line (such as ragged edges) or the emotional "turbulent feelings" attached to a particular flow or terminal node; a violent, haphazard or disharmonious commotion (such as in the ebb of gusts and lulls of wind action).

validation : a reinforcement of agreements or considerations as being "real."

viewpoint : see *"point-of-view"* (POV).

willingness : the state of conscious Self-determined ability and interest (directed attention) to *Be*, *Do* or *Have*; a Self-determined consideration to reach, face up to (*confront*) or manage some "mass" or energy; the extent to which an individual considers themselves able to participate, act or communicate along some line, to put attention or intention on the line, or to produce (create) an effect.

ZU : the ancient Sumerian cuneiform sign for the archaic verb—*"to know," "knowingness"* or *"awareness"*; in *Mardukite Zuism and Systemology*, the active energy/matter of the "Spiritual Universe" (AN) experienced as a *Lifeforce* or *consciousness* that imbues living forms extant in the "Physical Universe" (KI); *"Spiritual Life Energy"*; energy demonstrated by the WILL of an actualized *Alpha-Spirit* in the "Spiritual Universe" (AN), which impinges its *Awareness* into the Physical Universe (KI), animating/controlling *Life* for its experience of *beta-existence* along an individual Alpha-Spirit's personal *Identity-continuum*, called a *ZU-line*.

Zu-Line : a theoretical construct in *Mardukite Zuism and Systemology* demonstrating *Spiritual*

192

Life Energy (*ZU*) as a personal individual "continuum" of Awareness interacting with all Spheres of Existence on the Standard Model of Systemology; a spectrum of potential variations and interactions of a monistic continuum or singular *Spiritual Life Energy* demonstrated on the Standard Model; an energetic channel of potential POV and "locations" of Beingness, demonstrated in early Systemology materials as an individual Alpha-Spirit's personal *Identity- continuum*, potentially connecting *Awareness* of *Self* with "*Infinity*" simultaneous with all points considered in existence; a symbolic demonstration of the "*Life-line*" on which *Awareness (ZU)* extends from the direction of the "Spiritual Universe" (AN) in its true original *alpha state* through an entire possible range of activity resulting in its *beta state* and control of a *genetic-entity* occupying the *Physical Universe (KI).*

Zu-**Vision** : the true and basic (*Alpha*) Point-of-View (perspective, POV) maintained by *Self* as *Alpha-Spirit* outside boundaries or considerations of the *Human Condition* and *exterior* to beta-existence reality agreements with the Physical Universe; a POV of Self *as* "a unit of Spiritual Awareness" that exists independent of a "body" and entrapment in a *Human Condition*; "spirit vision" in its truest sense.

193

Collector's Edition Hardcover

THE FUNDAMENTALS OF
SYSTEMOLOGY

A Basic Course developed by
Joshua Free

*collecting material of six lesson-booklets
together in one volume!*

"Being More Than Human"

"Realities in Agreement"

"Windows To Experience"

"Ancient Systemology"

"A History of Systemology"

"Systemology Processing"

All *six* lesson-booklets of the first official
Basic Course on Mardukite Systemology
are combined together in *one volume* as
"Fundamentals of Systemology."

Lesson booklets are also available individually!

Collector's Edition Hardcover

THE PATHWAY TO
ASCENSION

The Systemology
Professional Course by
Joshua Free

All sixteen lessons available in two volumes!

"Increasing Awareness"

"Thought & Emotion"

"Clear Communication"

"Handling Humanity"

"Free Your Spirit"

"Escaping Spirit-Traps"

"Eliminating Barriers"

"Conquest of Illusion"

...and more!

All *sixteen* lesson-booklets of the newest
Professional Course on Mardukite Systemology
are combined together in *two volumes* as
"The Pathway to Ascension."

Lesson booklets are also available individually!

THE SYSTEM

Seekers and students of the *Professional Course* and *Advanced Training Course* will also be interested in the original *Systemology Core Research Series*. These *8* volumes are a complete chronological record of *Mardukite NexGen New Thought* developments published by the *Systemology Society* from 2019 through 2023.

The Systemology Core series begins with the first professional publication released when our *Mardukite Systemology* emerged from the underground in 2019, with: *"The Tablets of Destiny Revelation."*

OLOGY CORE

The Tablets of Destiny Revelation:
*How Long-Lost Anunnaki Wisdom
Can Change the Fate of Humanity*

Crystal Clear: *Handbook for Seekers*

Metahuman Destinations (*2 volumes*)

Imaginomicon:
Approaching Gateways to Higher Universes

Way of the Wizard: *Utilitarian Systemology*

Systemology-180: *Fast-Track to Ascension*

Systemology Backtrack:
Reclaiming Spiritual Power & Past-Life Memory

PUBLISHED BY THE **JOSHUA FREE** IMPRINT REPRESENTING

The Mardukite Academy of Systemology

THE JOSHUA FREE IMPRINT
JFI PUBLICATIONS

MARDUKITE
ZUISM

mardukite.com

www.ingramcontent.com/pod-product-compliance
Lightning Source LLC
Chambersburg PA
CBHW061154120626
46546CB00005B/2059